Spanner and Pen:

Post-War Memoirs

Roy Fuller

Spanner and Pen

POST-WAR MEMOIRS

SINCLAIR-STEVENSON

First published in Great Britain by
Sinclair-Stevenson Limited
7/8 Kendrick Mews
London SW7 3HG, England

Copyright © 1991 by Roy Fuller

British Library Cataloguing in Publication Data
A CIP catalogue record for this book is available
from the British Library.
ISBN 1 85619 040 4

Typeset by Rowland Phototypesetting Limited
Bury St Edmunds, Suffolk
Printed and bound in Great Britain by
Clays Limited, St Ives plc

Well, since you're from the other side of town,
I'll tell you how I hold a soft job down.
In the designing-rooms and laboratory
I'm dressed in overalls, and so pretend
To be on business from the factory.
The workmen think I'm from the other end.
The in-betweens and smart commission-men
Believe I must have some pull with the boss.
So, playing off the spanner against the pen,
I never let the rumour get across
Of how I am no use at all to either,
And draw the pay of both for doing neither.

Norman Cameron: 'Public-House Confidence'

LIST OF ILLUSTRATIONS

To Julian Symons
who courageously renounced the spanner
but resisted the bogus

ACKNOWLEDGEMENTS

For permission to publish extracts the author and publishers wish to acknowledge the following:

'Public-house Confidence' from *Collected Poems and Selected Translations* by Norman Cameron, eds Warren Hope and Jonathan Barker (Anvil Press Poetry 1990)
Collected Poems by Herbert Read (David Higham Associates Ltd)
'Devonshire Street W1' from *Collected Poems* by John Betjeman (John Murray Publishers Ltd)
Opus Posthumous by Wallace Stevens (Faber & Faber Ltd 1990)
Robert Graves letter (A P Watt & Son)

Special thanks are due to the following:
To Georgina Dobrée for the poem by her mother
To Patrick Hamilton for the poem by his father
To Patricia Ledward for the extract from the poem by her
To Monica Pudney for the extract from the poem by John Pudney

CONTENTS

I

THE END OF THE FORTIES

I CAME out of the Navy in 1946 possessing two suits of clothes, plus the 'hacking jacket' and grey trousers picked up at Olympia as part of the civilian outfit made available to all servicemen on demobilization. One of the suits even pre-dated my joining the Woolwich in December 1938. Made of dark-brown Manx tweed, laboriously chosen, it had always been a favourite of mine. In a novel I had to abandon when called up in April 1941, I had clad my dapper hero in it. During Navy years it had been attacked by moths, but in 1946 I had it 'invisibly mended', a service still available at a modest price, in which patient ladies darned the holes with threads drawn from interior seams of the garment in question. The other suit was of a thicker but still plain tweed, of a subdued green, the colour nevertheless quite *avant garde* for its time. This had been stout enough to survive the war intact. Two suits of such antiquity were plainly inadequate for the resumed life of a lawyer, and I eventually went to a quite small shop called Austin's at the bottom of Shaftesbury Avenue with the intention of buying another off the peg. I must have seen in the window something that took my fancy. It was a shop that later, possibly even at that time, sold shirts from the USA with button-down collars, and other items of a quite novel or show-biz character, appropriate to its location. It was run by two men I took to be Jewish brothers, though one was bald, the other gingerish; agreeable, but unlikely to let someone escape who had set foot over their threshold. On this occasion it turned out they had nothing to fit me that I liked. I succumbed to their offer to make a suit for me. My hesitation may have been on account of the price, probably anticipated more than actual. But I was pleased with the product that emerged. The material was a soft, grey, herringbone tweed, the coat cut longer in the body than any suit I had ever had – in fact, in the style familiar from American films of the day – the middle button of the three, the one intended to be fastened, situated accurately in the waist. Did I think the trousers slightly too wide, the two pleats at either side of the waist-band too generous? Not to begin with, I feel sure, but fashion changed in those regards.

Certainly I came to possess two suits for which I had much less affection. Clothes rationing was still in force, and my mother, in the north, had acquired a suit-length on the black market. I had it made up by the sort of tailor willing to work on such extraneous material. I chose a double-breasted style, but the coat was ungenerous in length, and the dark-blue cloth itself of indifferent quality. Parsimony and compassion for my mother's enterprise compelled me to persevere with the thing until it could be decently interred. The other suit that I wore with misgiving was a much superior affair, but in truth it was too big. My brother gave it to me when he departed for a tour of duty in Singapore, as totally unsuitable for the climate anticipated. During the war he had served in the catering branch of the RAF, had been persuaded (with promise of rapid promotion) to stay on in peacetime. Immediately before Singapore he had been at the Air Ministry: hence the civilian suit, which he had had made at Simpson's in Piccadilly; nutty, like all his garments. Proof that I wore it on more than everyday occasions is afforded by a photograph in *Picture Post* of 19 February 1949, which shows me with the poet Laurie Lee, eating some snack, garbed in the suit in question. But surely anyone interested in sartorial matters can deduce that the suit was not made for me.

At a rather later date, I too had a suit made at Simpson's, a distinct success – double-breasted, like the black-market affair, but properly cut, and in dark-grey flannel, a material not then the New York executive *cliché* it subsequently became. However, thereafter, until I retired as solicitor to the Woolwich Equitable Building Society – when I ceased to wear suits as a diurnal practice, and had accumulated enough to last me through the formal occasions of the rest of my life (unless they were amazingly prolonged) – I patronized the ample ready-made department of Aquascutum at the bottom of Regent Street. Suffering, then unbeknown to me, from hyperthyroidism, I had lost weight, but Aquascutum did a 'young man's fitting', the thirty-seven-inch chest size which usually fitted me without alteration. (Incidentally, Aquascutum, like Burberry's, had, as the name indicates, originally been celebrated for raincoats: in his immediate post-First War diaries Siegfried Sassoon refers to an Aquascutum as familiarly as he might a Burberry, and indeed there is a similar reference in A. C. Benson's journal for 1902. So it is odd the word is not in the OED, even the Supplement.)

Apropos of Austin's, that portion of Shaftesbury Avenue was also familiar through visiting the Trocadero opposite, part of the J. Lyons & Co empire, like the Regent Palace Hotel nearby, in which conglomerate my brother had done some of his training before the war. For a spell he had accompanied the Lyons meat buyer to Smithfield, and I had been impressed by his telling me how the best meat had been insisted upon for the Lyons hotels. Occasionally, I must have just gone into the Troc for a drink, because I remember seeing in the deserted lounge, at a fairly early hour of the morning, Sid Field talking earnestly to a lady I doubt was his wife. (Sid Field died prematurely: some of his comic routines are preserved on film but give no idea how laughter-achingly funny he was 'live', in contact with the audience that night after night packed the Prince of Wales Theatre to see the series of revues in which he starred, all at once promoted to West End fame from a long apprenticeship in provincial music-halls.) Later, it may have been that lounge that was turned into a restaurant, still under the aegis of the Troc, named the 'Salted Almond' – the *décor* modern, especially compared with the traditional Troc appearance, and the menu on the whole light, suitable for women shoppers, and executives wanting to break out of the chop-house mould. But my patronizing it surely indicates a lingering provincial attitude to the West End.

The sight of the private Sid Field making such an impression

– and, indeed, the whole business of those Kleinian Good and Bad suits – brings home to me, writing towards the end of 1988, the extraordinary remoteness of the first post-war years. In his excellent book of 'autobiographies', *Time and Time Again*, Dan Jacobson describes the London of those days as it seemed to a South African new-arrival:

> There were times when I felt that an inward dissolution would do as effectively over a wider area what the bombs had done where they had fallen, and that the blackened, gutted hulks of houses one saw everywhere were the condition towards which the whole city was slowly, inevitably sinking. The public buildings were filthy, pitted with shrapnel scars, running with pigeon dung from every coign and eave; eminent statesmen and dead kings of stone looked out upon the world with soot-blackened faces, like coons in a grotesque carnival; bus tickets and torn newspapers blew down the streets or lay in white heaps in the parks; cats bred in the bomb-sites, where people flung old shoes, tin cans, and cardboard boxes; whole suburbs of private houses were peeling, cracking, crazing, their windows unwashed, their steps unswept, their gardens untended; innumerable little cafés reeked of chips frying in stale fat . . .

I doubt if we who had lived in London during the latter year or so of the war felt all this anything like so acutely; in fact, the West End and many of the suburbs seem to me now more squalid than they did then. Yet certainly the joy at the war being over, interrupted life resumed, a Labour government voted in, was tempered by a number of factors difficult now to recover in their intensity. Foremost was the conviction that a Third World War was quite on the cards, an atomic conflict between the late allies, the Soviet Union and the West. And perhaps in other cases than my own was the sense that, after all, one wanted more than the simple return to pre-war existence; that the *boule-versements* of the war should have resulted in the leading of a 'different' life; in my case the achievement of a higher level of artistic creativity – in the famous words of Henry James (which in fact one read for the first time when the *Notebooks* were published in 1947): 'To live *in* the world of creation – to get into it and stay in it – to frequent it and haunt it – to *think* intently and fruitfully – to woo combinations and inspirations into being by a depth and continuity of attention and meditation – this is the only thing . . .' But that one never achieved this was in fact due as much to lack of genius as of opportunity in the life embraced.

2

Addressing envelopes in Labour Party committee rooms in the 1945 General Election was the only direct form of political action undertaken since I left Blackpool in the mid-Thirties. 'I'm overfond of Uncle Joe', I wrote in the dedicatory poem of my collection of 1949, *Epitaphs and Occasions*, but the verb was really determined by the metre: 'Too lenient to Uncle Joe' would have been more accurate. In the immediate post-war years I still sympathized with the Soviets; thought the 1917 Revolution a gain not to be surrendered, despite its plainly having gone awry. Strange to relate, the crimes of the Stalin era had not really made their mark on me: the idea of bourgeois propaganda or the notion of the 'necessary murder' still prevailed over the evidence coming in. Because of this, and the alarm about another war, I became a member of the Society for Cultural Relations with the USSR; indeed, served on its committee. I suppose in America 'the SCR' would have been labelled a Communist Party front organization, but it was not so in any conspiratorial sense. For instance, we sent a quarterly selection of new English books to our Soviet counterpart (or the Writers' Union, I forget), the choice being free from political bias, in fact positively challenging censorship. When a delegation of writers came from the USSR – including the (then or subsequently) notorious *apparatchik* Surkov – I remember asking them why the fiction they sent us was always ideologically simplistic; why didn't we receive 'neurotic' novels? The question betrays my naivety, but it was also typical of the 'cultural relations' we were trying to establish. (Incidentally, we had better visitors than Surkov: I recall being in a group round Pudovkin – whose films I had gone to great lengths to catch in

5

the Thirties – feeling a sense of awe; but what fell from his lips has gone from mind. He was of ordinary, not to say commonplace appearance, absolutely not acting the great man.)

Indeed, most SCR activity has been blanketed by time. Compton Mackenzie was President (or whatever the figurehead was called). I see him at some gathering half seated on a table, silver, brilliantined hair brushed straight back, grey imperial beard wagging as he gassed. In my youth I had borrowed from the Blackpool Public Library, and read with absorption, the *Sinister Street* series and other novels: at the SCR he was to me still a figure of charisma, though I had long moved away from the kind of literature he represented. I suppose if confronted with a list of my colleagues on the SCR committee memories would return: little has stuck – though I easily summon up David Magarshack, man of sound views, likeable, though with the dogged irritability of some character in the Dostoevsky he translated so well.

Presumably it was through the SCR that other leftish characters entered my life. The threat of a Third World War became so acute that there were several small *ad hoc* meetings of writers to take some action, perhaps somewhat Learish ('What they are, yet I know not, but they shall be / The terrors of the earth'). Private houses were the venue: into one such meeting came one night Reggie Smith and his wife Olivia Manning, between them a half-comatose individual who, dormouse-like, sat between them but added nothing to the proceedings, and was later discovered to be Dylan Thomas. How amazed I should have been then had I been told I should live through more or less peaceful times into the second half of my seventies (to say nothing of the amazement that Dylan Thomas should continue to be thought a 'great' poet). How wise and farseeing was Tony Powell about this time to embark upon *A Dance to the Music of Time*. Even had I been capable of a long work I should have been too pessimistic to start the thing until a time arrived when age would have made it too late. Besides, a native impatience or anxiety has always urged me to finish a task quickly.

3

In my previous memoirs, *The Strange and the Good*, two characters figured prominently – Marston and Waller. Both I had known in schooldays, both reappeared in early adult life, with greatest effect during the two periods I had in London at law crammers as an articled clerk. Their subsequent destinies I left to be retailed later – if at all, for when I had reached the point of demobilization from the Navy I brought the memoirs to an end, with no intention of going on.

I heard from my brother that Gilbert Waller had in fact materialized sensationally towards the end of the war in the olive drabs of an American officer (rather like the non-combatant Auden, though in Waller's case he had not to travel to the USA to escape call-up, for his Umkaloabo-cured TB must have sufficiently prevented that eventuality). Waller, a journalist, had been English correspondent, possibly a mere stringer, of a Chicago newspaper, then achieved war-correspondent status when Europe was opened up. Later, in the early Fifties, through one of the coincidences that have marked my brother's life, he found that Waller was a near neighbour of his in Chiswick, where by chance he had gone to live. By then Waller was married to his second wife; the young man who had disseminated sneezing-powder in the pubs along the Gray's Inn Road transformed to a *paterfamilias*. I myself saw him playing – characteristically overacting – that role. One Guy Fawkes Night my wife and I were invited, with my brother and his family, round to the Wallers' house. The setting-off of fireworks was accompanied by the eating of parkin and treacle toffee, tradition of Waller's Lancashire childhood whose revival seemed somewhat precious, given Waller's unorthodox past. Not long after this, his wife ran away with the local vicar.

It was an astonishing turn, for Waller had always appeared a master of the amatory side of life, certainly by his own account. Equally surprising was his subsequent return to his home town of Blackpool, roots seemingly permanently pulled up long before in favour of a thoroughly metropolitan existence. No doubt, with his children, he needed the help of his mother, highly capable in domestic affairs, as indicated by the inculcation of the Bonfire Night routine. In due course he married yet again, a woman of property, presumably including shop property, for he was reported sitting idly outside an emporium selling (*inter alia*) picture postcards. This news came *via* Norman Lees, who had been engrossing clerk when I was an articled clerk, and who knew Gilbert Waller in his eccentric days of yore. Finally, Lees reported Waller's death, at no great age. Arnold Bennett could have made a novel of this life.

Marston had returned to Blackpool at a much earlier date, in fact before the war, abandoning the London advertising world, and entering his father's business, which was (I think mainly, if not solely) the manufacture of 'confectioners' egg', a substance used by bakers in cake-making and the like. He had gone back with a bride, a lady of his *louche* Bloomsbury days, thought unlikely to become such a fixture. The establishment he set up in his native town had the shabby pretensions of his own personal appearance – a sofa in black upholstery, stained by the processes of infants, springs to mind from the only visit I made. The judgement is not meant to be disparaging, though Marston's cleverness, eloquence, undoubted if ill-defined ability (to say nothing of his left-wing activities) seemed to have run into the sand.

But the war proved to inaugurate a sensational amelioration of his fortunes. The manufacture of confectioners' egg was judged vital to the war effort, and Marston was exempted from call-up. At some stage his father died: Marston ran the firm and presumably took the major share of the profits. I doubt I saw him during the war, but shortly thereafter he appeared one evening at our Blackheath flat. With him was a girl we had known well in the past, as the wife of someone other. They had been conveyed from their hotel in the West End in a taxi. (Marston's wife had perished through misadventure some time before.) In his familiar overbearing way, Marston had us all driven to the local pub, and (the taxi remaining at his command) arranged a meeting the next night at the Gargoyle Club, to us merely a notorious name. My present mind boggles that I should have fallen in with all this.

We dined at the Gargoyle, even in that matter Marston

imposing his will by pre-ordering the dishes served. Afterwards he caused a bottle of gin (and I think also of whisky) to be placed on the table: at any rate, there was a superfluity of booze to my frugal way of thinking. Did we dance? It may be so. At that date music was provided by Buddy Featherstonehaugh and his band, quite well known, an outfit that would have appealed to Marston, a jazz *aficionado*. The evening proved to be not entirely wasted: when I came to write *Fantasy and Fugue* (1954), the Corydon Club and the bandleader, Sonny Frankland, were founded on the Gargoyle and Featherstonehaugh.

I don't think one marvelled overmuch at Marston's lavish life-style (evidence of which came to us additionally to the London visit), for food shortage persisted, the demand for such dubious products as confectioners' egg presumably still strong. Then we heard that he was in trouble with the Inland Revenue. Most of his acquaintances must have been sympathetic or at least tactful, but when his old friend Waller called on him, the former's opening words, uttered not without relish, were: 'Well, you *are* in the shit, aren't you?' Though this confrontation came to us second-hand, one could visualize Waller on the doorstep, trenchcoat open, carrying a walking-stick, and blinking owlishly – characteristic image from the days when I, too, had helped to waft sneezing-powder into the nostrils of quiet drinkers on the edge of Bloomsbury. The tax fraud earned Marston a spell in prison, though his prosperity seemed not much affected, and he survived Waller by a good few years in the Channel Isles, where the Inland Revenue's fell hand did not extend. This life would have been rather beyond Arnold Bennett's scope.

4

I write this two days after the day on which my mother would have been a hundred years old – 28 October 1988. Would she have envisaged my remembering the anniversary? She once told my wife Kate that when I lived at home I too rarely spoke to her. There was no conflict, no tension: it simply was that during a prolonged adolescence I evolved no easy way of communicating with others, including her. I felt the problems of her health (she suffered for years from undiagnosed hyperthyroidism); her widowed state; her eking out, to give her two sons a good start in life, the far from ample inheritance from my dead father. Whether she realized the depth of this feeling, I do not know. After the war she remarried, a widower somewhat younger than herself, of modest status, and went to live in the cottage he rented in a village outside Huddersfield. Particularly after her long widowhood, it was an unexpected step, and one wondered if happiness would ensue. My stepfather's devotion ensured this, though it proved of brief duration, for my mother contracted cancer, and died in 1949. Because of her remarriage I was largely spared the harrowing progress of the disease. Before it was diagnosed it was plain her digestion was not in order: on a visit I noticed charcoal biscuits in a drawer and other slight signs. Then, when she faced surgery, I went up again. A colostomy was on the cards: in her hospital bed she said to me: 'I've always dreaded that.' It had prefigured my father's end, which had come after great suffering nearly thirty years before. My mother and stepfather, hands clasped, tears in eyes, seemed all at once much younger than me.

But a colostomy was not performed. Reading between the lines, it was evident that matters had gone too far even for that, though my stepfather, as later we walked away through the hospital grounds, advanced a dubiously medical hope that surgical success had been achieved in some other way. He took me for high tea to a marvellous place of pre-war standards, impossible to find in the south, where soundly-dressed Huddersfield businessmen were tucking into steak and chips, plaice and chips, and the like, served by motherly or embryo motherly waitresses. I suppose we enjoyed the food, though since the diagnosis of my mother's cancer I had felt a pain lurking behind all of life. But I don't think this was directly connected with the finding, not long after that visit to Huddersfield, that my own ancient digestive trouble was a duodenal ulcer: pain had driven me to my GP and thence to X-ray.

I was only too conscious during the long weeks of my mother's terminal illness that my duty was to make the journey to the cottage to see her. Characteristically, I feared the encounter too greatly. I even dreaded the regular telephone call to my stepfather. At that epoch I had bought the discs of Milhaud's *Scaramouche*, catchy suite for two pianos, then not at all well known. I often played them, though the pleasure derived was peculiarly tinctured by sadness and concern.

Then came the telephone conversation constantly dreaded. My mother was 'in a bad way' or perhaps 'poor way', my stepfather said. When I replied I would come at once, he took that for granted. Ghastly journey, by train and bus (we were not to own a motor car until 1951), trying to steel myself for what lay in wait. When at last I confronted my mother on her death-bed, I said to my stepfather: 'I don't know how you stood it.' We came downstairs: high tea on this occasion was steamed fish – my mother's elder sister, Edith (who had nobly come to help out in my mother's final days), having been advised that I was on the bland diet then fashionable for the treatment of peptic ulcers. The fish was short of salt, perhaps overcooked – the incongruous memory survives. My mother would not have been surprised, always taking a critical view of Edith's domestic capabilities, her own of a high standard.

My mother died the next night: for me a release none too soon. Some of the emotion of the event is caught by 'Ten Memorial Poems', reprinted in *New and Collected Poems 1934–84*. I have never thought of it till this moment, but my mother's death marked the end of the Forties – strange decade, which began, as it were, in the Thirties; actualizing the long-dreaded war, and the conflict with fascism, and ending, so it proved, with a dud social revolution, and the start for me of a fairly steady and greatly more productive life of writing verse, and, indeed, prose.

Most poets want to change their style as the years roll by, as well as wanting to get better. I feel that in modest terms this happened to me in 1954, not least as a result of a letter from Robert Graves. I can't bring back at this date the reason for my sending him a collection of poems called *Counterparts* I published in that year. I did not know him, and so far as I recall did not meet him until I sat next to him at a luncheon given by his publisher when he was awarded the Queen's Gold Medal for Poetry in 1968. The result anyway was a letter (10 September 1954) that impressed me greatly. I quote some of it that concerns *Counterparts*:

> Thank you most kindly for the poems, the first of yours I have read in bulk: the 'verse as thick and coiled as bowels', [a quotation from the book] oppressed, stoical, humorous, on the whole very well written indeed: no 'chancing your arm' . . .
>
> But what a world you live in! Stoicism indeed seems the only possible attitude. The word 'love' does not occur even to be saluted with a witty Bronx cheer. Nor any woman but Lizzie Eustace [from a Trollope novel mentioned in the book] and the Witch . . .
>
> Your solicitor's job doesn't sound very thrilling . . .

I don't suppose the last quoted sentence cheered me up any less than some of the rest, but by 1954 a better alternative to a career in the law was absolutely not on the cards. What did strike home was Graves pointing out the absence of the White Goddess and her powers, and, behind his praise, the reproach of having a too-canny attitude to the subjects and forms of verse. It was true I had been happily married for getting on for twenty years, and my directly amatory poems (awful) pre-dated even my first published book of poems. But Graves's letter made me see that quite unconsciously I had been excluding too much from my verse, and that accordingly (or in addition) it lacked ambition. As a result, I believe my next book, *Brutus's Orchard* (1957) marked an advance; in particular, some poems evaded the 'oppressed, stoical, humorous' persona by being in effect dramatic monologues (including the piece that drew Dame Edith Sitwell's scorn, 'Autobiography of a Lungworm'). I also thought my verse took another turn in *New Poems* (1968), though I wish my excursion there into syllabic verse had waited until I had met Robert Bridges's daughter, Elizabeth Daryush, during my Oxford professorship, when (gormless, as so often, theretofore) I appreciated for the first time the importance in syllabics of the end-stopped line, and even of rhyme, as will later appear.

II

RECOLLECTIONS OF THE
BLACKHEATH POETS

I

THE Woolwich Equitable Building Society, though when I joined its staff in 1938 was already well on the way to becoming a national institution, still had its headquarters in Woolwich (where it was founded in 1847), a mainly industrial and commercial area of south-east London. Two or three miles to the west is Blackheath, a residential suburb, looking green on the map, which is why, in my then ignorance of London suburbia, I chose it to find accommodation for myself, my wife and infant son on taking up my new post. The war soon interrupted our early married life, but in 1945 we all returned to Blackheath, and early in 1946 I resumed my pre-war occupation with the Woolwich (or the Equitable, as the locals called it).

Before the war I had started to publish poems in little magazines, though my job as a lawyer and utter lack of fame prevented me from leading any sort of literary life, even had I wanted to. I had formed an enduring friendship with Julian Symons, then a poet and little-magazine editor, later a notable critic and author of crime novels, and through him had become acquainted with a few fairly minor Thirties poets like Gavin Ewart, H. B. Mallalieu and Ruthven Todd. But in no sense did I move in 'literary circles'. I may well have known – in fact, I believe I did know – that Blackheath was the home of Charles Madge (in those pre-war days a poet whose relative eminence I would not have attempted to approach) and Kathleen Raine (a poet of scarcely less *réclame*). But they, and any other poetic residents, remained unknown, unseen.

Post-war, all was changed. For one thing, Julian Symons and his wife (through my knowing of the vacancy in a time of housing shortage) took the top-floor flat in a large Victorian house where we occupied the ground-floor flat. Also, I had brought out two wartime books of verse with modest success, and after the war began to publish prose fiction. So that when a number of *littérateurs*, each celebrated in his own way, came to live in Blackheath, it was perhaps not surprising that I eventually came across them.

Blackheath was a rather unfashionable suburb before the war. In 1938 the estate agents offered us a selection of flats at rentals around £1. 5s. a week. Its architecture, mainly Victorian but with a substratum of Georgian, had by and large decayed. After the war, steeply rising prices in desirable north-of-the-river districts caused many discriminating accommodation-seekers to look southwards, and Blackheath began to go up in the world, particularly as its war-damaged buildings were repaired and brought back into use. Among the discriminating were some intellectuals.

After the rarely edifying journey from central London along the New and Old Kent Roads, the way rises steeply from the squalor of Deptford to the heath of Blackheath, an open area of grassland bordered by on the whole interesting domestic architecture, some distinguished. The openness is augmented by the contiguous Greenwich Park, descending from the heath almost to the Thames. A poet who lived at Blackheath in the Eighteen-Nineties has given a good idea, in a poem called 'A Nocturne at Greenwich', of the atmosphere and topography of this ambience. The poet was Victor Plarr, now remembered, if at all, as the original of 'Monsieur Verog' in Ezra Pound's *Hugh Selwyn Mauberley* – the 'Plarr talking of mathematics' of *The Pisan Cantos*.

> Far out, beyond my window, in the gloom
> 　　Nightly I see thee loom,
> Thou vast black city. Oh, but night is kind
> 　　Here where Thames' waters wind,
> To the grim formless features of thy face.

They do assume such grace
In the deep darkness, starred through leagues of night,
  With long streets, fringed with light,
Or with the lanthorns of the ships that aye
  Ascend the water-way . . .
Up from the darkness echoes sleepily
  The shipman's wandering cry,
Or, like a wild beast's call heard in a dream,
  The siren's undulant scream
Whistles the darkling midnight through and through,
  While with her labouring screw
Some dim leviathan of ships drops down
  Past storied Greenwich town . . .
Past the great hospital she drops, and past
  The marshes, still and vast,
Below the lines of Woolwich and the lines
  Of Bostal's shadowy pines,
On to that world of Saxon brine and fen,
  Old races, vanished men,
Where Thames, from heron-haunted shores set free,
  Merges in northern sea.
Here, in my chamber, 'mong my books, at peace,
  I watch thee without cease,
Thou ancient stream, mysterious as the sky
  Which starless glooms on high.
About me, on the volume-peopled wall,
  The famed old authors all
Sleep their just sleep, and in the hearth's clear beams
  Dante's medallion gleams,
And Brutus and great Tully o'er the shelves
  Commune among themselves.
This silent music of what once hath been
  Suits well with that night scene:
Nay, its essential sweetness sweeter grows,
  Because that river flows
Through northern midnight, big with life and doom,
  Out yonder in the gloom.

That is the Greenwich side, my side, of Blackheath: on the opposite or south side lies Blackheath Village, so called from ancient times, with its shops and railway station – a stop on the Southern Railway, as it was known before nationalization, nineteen minutes from Charing Cross, much less from London Bridge.

Bonamy Dobrée came to live near the Village when he retired in the early Fifties from his professorship in English Literature at Leeds University. Joe Ackerley, finding that Bonamy and I were separated only by the heath, said to me I ought to get to know him. I feel sure I made no move myself to obey this behest. I can't be said to have been at any time of my life keen to extend my acquaintances, and in Bonamy's case I would have been diffident about imposing myself on him. He was not only a distinguished academic and anthologist, whose work was well known even outside the scholarly world; he had also in 1935 been joint author of a book which at the time made a great impression on me – *The Floating Republic*, an account of the mutinies in the Royal Navy in 1797. In the early Thirties I had been deeply committed to left-wing politics, the ideas of Marxism, suddenly come upon, seeming utterly revelatory. Lenin's *State and Revolution*, for instance, I saw as incontrovertible, the apparatus of army, police and the courts the means of keeping imposed a bourgeois regime on the more numerous and less privileged proletariat. But how could the power of this apparatus, particularly the armed forces, be broken so as to allow the take-over of the state by the working class? It seemed a quite impossible event, in Britain at any rate, where the repressive machine was so well disciplined. *The Floating Republic* gave an inkling of how it might come about. It had to recount the final defeat of the mutineers, but its sympathy with their ideas and personalities made vivid an early example of working-class enterprise and solidarity, and gave hope to the left in the grim days of the Thirties' economic crisis.

But however it happened, my wife and I came to know Bonamy and his wife. Valentine Dobrée was a dark, Mediterranean-type, three years younger than Bonamy, who was born in 1891. Accomplished paintings by her hung on the walls of their house, though by the time of meeting her she had abandoned oils for *collages*. Eventually it came out (or perhaps I read somewhere) that in earlier days she had published several prose works, and in due course I discovered in the London Library a novel of hers called, strikingly enough, *Your Cuckoo Sings By Kind*. She had a further literary surprise in store: in 1965 Faber & Faber brought out a collection of her verse, *This Green Tide*. Though the book was far from negligible, no doubt her appearance in a list with such fashionable figures as Auden, Larkin and Ted Hughes was due to Bonamy's long friendship with T. S. Eliot, the Faber director with the poetry say-so. Perhaps I may quote an entire poem to give some notion of the collection's quality:

The Enchantment of Raquel Meller

The fragrance of violets was more potent than violets,
Dark-mantled flowers, full of false modesty,
Their pungency distilled, bottled and advertised
To create bewilderment in men, adding mystery
And illusive charm to the ladies,
Suggesting limits of discreet seduction.
A birthday gift for Mamma
Disdainful of patchouli:
More homely than lilies.

When in Paris, City of Discovery far in the 'twenties,
That rare singer, Raquel, peddled violets.
The freshness of her voice and presence,
A song of violets, shocked the long-corrupted air;
The hot excitement of the late night performance
– Back to lost childhood and its own innocence –
Awoke confusion in the heart of youth deprived,
Gave benison to a shell-shocked generation,
Ousting stale odours, shaming the lechers,
Knitting those who had been taken apart.
Strange props for the halls,
The cordials and simples of an old healing art

Borne in a plain reeded basket
By a bewitching deceiver.
Her knacks, small bunches of button-hole flowers;
With her distilling, the aroma of violets
Became more poignant than violets.

It was even more of a surprise when a few years after
Valentine's death I read in Virginia Woolf's *Diary* of Valentine's
part in the Partridge/Carrington/Brenan amatory mix-up at the
period of the poem I have quoted, for in the years when we
knew them Bonamy and Valentine were a singularly devoted
couple. During the latter part of that time Valentine was more
or less an invalid, Bonamy head cook and bottle-washer. To this
day my wife will refer to Bonamy's virtuous morning habit of
taking the newspapers to Valentine's bed, and getting in it to
read and discuss the news with her.

Valentine had an easy and amiable conversational style, yet
one frequently lost the thread of her argument on any subject
save the simplest. Some of her poems betray the same difficulty,
but of course that is what one has become used to encountering
on the printed poetic page. Orally, it was best to assent to her
recondite propositions, try to bring the exchanges nearer earth.

Valentine's darkness formed a contrast to Bonamy's silver
hair and moustache. His slim, erect figure added to the military
impression conveyed – indeed, not misleadingly, for he had
once been in the regular Army, and served with distinction in
both the German wars. In the Second World War, Virginia
Woolf noted him as 'Spick and span, clipped, grey, with a
rainbow of medal ribbons across his breast' (*Diary*, 6 April
1940). He took up his post at Leeds University in the mid-
Thirties, and returned there after the war. One of his early
pupils was Richard Hoggart, later to become famous as (*inter
alia*) the author of *The Uses of Literacy*. In the early Sixties, for
a *Festschrift* in Bonamy's honour, Hoggart wrote a remarkable
account of his relations with his master, illuminating both men
(a somewhat different version appears in volume one of Hoggart's autobiography). To begin to quote from it would be fatal,
for every word is telling. But one thing particularly emerges,

pointed by Hoggart's origins in an utterly different society –
Bonamy was quintessentially Cambridge and upper middle-
class, tempered by the generally leftish intellectualism of the
Bloomsbury epoch. All this was allied with a sort of inspecting
Army's officer's sharp regard for neatness, cleanliness, good
behaviour, and tradition. No doubt it was his deep-dyed leftism
that prompted his support, often of a practical nature (and by
no means discouraged by Valentine) of poets and painters. He
bought and read books of new verse, and when I first knew him
had paid a young painter to contribute unskilled help in the
garden. Valentine's patronage once brought notoriety in the
local newspaper: at a show by the Blackheath Art Society she
purchased a sculpture, essentially a small, upright, wooden
member, with an aperture near the top *à la* Henry Moore,
mounted on a modest base. It subsequently emerged that the
'sculpture' had been a piece of firewood, the aperture a knot-
hole; that anyone should pay a guinea or two for this was
derided in the newspaper. But Valentine spiritedly defended
her purchase, said she liked it, firewood though it may have
been.

In the early days of our knowing them we were invited to a
large Christmas party, a good proportion of the guests being
their daughter Georgina's young friends, though some of the
proceedings seeming to hark back to the Twenties, if not
earlier. Gambling games went on, but the stakes – a large
amount of copper coin distributed equally among the guests –
were provided by (and eventually lost or, I think, returned to)
the 'house', so that the pleasure and pain of winning and losing
was divorced from financial advantage or anxiety. The climax of
the party involved Bonamy's sudden appearance in evening-
dress, with top-hat and cane, to make (I forget what) some
announcement or speech, an event undeniably effective,
though not without faint embarrassment to an uncommitted
onlooker.

The house the Dobrées bought in Blackheath where this took
place was rather misleadingly called Wemyss Cottage, since it
was a commodious villa, with extensive outbuildings and a
garden that ran downhill a long way to an adjoining road, Pond

Road. In those days Georgina was still at home, so that the house was not too commodious. When we first knew them she was just making her way as a professional clarinettist (doubling enterprisingly on the basset-horn), and later became professor at the Royal Academy of Music. I think it was after the Dobrées' purchase that the Borough Council filled in the pond and marshy land in Pond Road opposite the rear of the Dobrées' garden, and created a housing estate in neo-Georgian style among the otherwise agreeable architecture. But Bonamy and Valentine, unlike most house-owners in the area, would not have seen this as anything other than to be accepted – even welcomed – *pro bono publico.*

To the *Festschrift* referred to, I contributed a set of couplets that bring in some of the foregoing themes:

Wemyss Cottage, 1956

A street of battered laisser faire
Leads to the house: past its parterre
Blushes the bogus-Georgian of
The Borough Council's awful love.
Thus the twin shadows of the State
Fall upon stucco, lawn and slate
And on the Afric god who smiles
Across the little Flemish tiles
To where a painter keeps alive
By helping with the spade. Birds strive
Against a clarinet's long curl
Swayed by the breathing of a girl.
From the professor peeps a slim
Volume of poetry – for him
Neither the best nor past's enough:
He really buys the newest stuff,
Indulgent with the private dream
Though longing for a public theme.
So often since that former song
Corporate decisions have been wrong.
Committees set to make a choice

Have mostly raised a stupid voice.
Now it's a marvel that there still
Remain good things for groups to kill.
Before such ambiguities
The poet only murmurs his,
Revulsed by almost every faction
And quite incapable of action.
Moved by the emblems here, his pen
Writes of the obvious again.
Magnolias offer on dead wood
Their tiny lip-sticked cups; the good
Inherent in briar starts to show
And what the tag says soon will blow.
The mistress of the house imparts
Nurture to soil in which the arts
Extend: the tendrils of a tune
Creep up the windows: in the noon
Hues leap from beds; and, ordered by
A critical hand, the shrubbery
Of verse (that flowers on gloomy caves)
Reminds the sense of all that raves.
The guest must take his leave at last
By the unequal way that's past
Or through the future's juster hell.
Precarious happiness, farewell!

These lines were originally written in heroic couplets, abandoned as utterly NBG. When a request to contribute to the *Festschrift* arrived, I shortened the lines and so made them just about publishable, given the geniality of the occasion; a lesson about poetic form. They are accurate in detail and therefore possibly worth exhuming. What is depicted comes back to me vividly as spring or summer evenings returning with Bonamy from some (more or less stupid) committee meeting in town either by train or, in early days, when parking was easier, in his motor car. At that epoch he and Valentine had a car each, neither of any distinction. As Richard Hoggart says, Bonamy 'would always buy only the cheapest serviceable car; it was

simply a means of getting quickly from here to there'. He was a
driver some of whose eccentricities I used when describing the
driving of the aged poet Daniel House in *The Carnal Island*,
absent-mindedness about the choke being a notable feature.

Yes, happy days – the house and garden full of interest,
Valentine still physically active, a glass or two of sherry and
always some tit-bits provided to go with them, often the clarinet
roulades in the background. Then time began to take its toll, as
I fear will often be recounted in these pages.

The last body Bonamy and I sat on together was the Board of
the Poetry Book Society. Bonamy had joined at the suggestion
of its secretary, Eric Walter White, the expert on Stravinsky and
Benjamin Britten. I remember thinking that Bonamy, for all his
enthusiasm for new poetry, was rather elderly to be asked to
serve, and, sure enough, since the meetings were held after
lunch, he now and then dropped off to sleep during the course
of them. But it may well have been that Eric's motive was to give
Bonamy an outside interest in his domesticated old age.

We would return by rail from the Arts Council's premises in
St James's Square, where the Board meetings were held, and
repair for a drink not to Wemyss Cottage but a house with the
Pond Road frontage which Bonamy and Valentine had built at
the end of the Wemyss Cottage garden. Valentine's health had
broken down, never to recover. The Pond Road house, modest
though it was, constituted a remarkable embodiment of their
idiosyncratic personalities and way of life. They had designed it
as essentially three large rooms: one for Valentine, one for
Bonamy, plus a large kitchen in which to eat as well as cook.
They had sold Wemyss Cottage and were saddened at certain
unaesthetic developments of it and its garden by subsequent
owners. The kind of unostentatious, cultivated life the Dobrées
expected the middle class to live had sunk further into decline.

Two expeditions made with Bonamy at this period remain in
mind. Regular poetry readings used to be held in an upper room
of a public-house in Dulwich called the Greyhound, an awkward journey by public transport from Blackheath. For some
reason – could I myself have been performing? – Bonamy and I
attended, driving there in my car. We were in good time (or

perhaps the start of proceedings was tardy, not unusual at such events), and there was sufficient margin for a number of drinks, most, if not all, bought by me, which rather suggests a reader taking the edge off his nerves. After the show there was a return to the bar. I was astonished, brought up to eschew mixing one's drinks, that on the occasion of each round Bonamy ordered a different beverage, eventually arriving at such comparative rarities as rum. It occurred to me that it was a regression to a former mode of behaviour, or possibly cementing the novelty of a 'night out'. At the end of the evening he was not in the least the worse for drink.

On the other occasion Bonamy had come by, perhaps bought, two tickets for a poetry reading in one of the South Bank halls by Edith Sitwell, and invited me to accompany him. Had I had less regard for Bonamy I would have declined, for at that time my opinion of the Dame was at its nadir. She was not, in any case, a good reader of verse. The memory that endures is of a rendering of the sleep-walking scene from *Macbeth*, in which she also read the names of the characters before each speech, an eminently prosaic procedure. (Lady Macbeth had been a favoured role of Edith Sitwell's for some time: in a letter to Nancy Mitford of 9 November 1950, Evelyn Waugh reported her as playing the part at the Museum of Modern Art in New York with 'Glenway Westcott as Banquo, David Horner in a tartan dinner-jacket as MacDuff. Lady Ribblesdale as the witches. Cheapest seats £5. I wish I could be there.') Bonamy accepted all that happened as he had accepted the range of alcohol on offer at the Greyhound. The vision comes to me of sitting in the interval outdoors by the Thames among the concrete, in the summer air, our exchanges not altogether fluent. I have never been a great conversationalist, certainly not unless my *vis-à-vis* shared some everyday life, quite far removed from literature and ideas.

Undoubtedly Valentine's ill-health limited the intercourse between Kate and myself and the Dobrées, and my sharing committee duties with Bonamy came to an end in the course of time. It must have been during my five years as Oxford's Professor of Poetry that I met Bonamy by chance in Blackheath

Village. Was it a prior intimation by some third party or simply through observing the signs of age (slight shabbiness, uncut hair, imperfect shaving, abstracted locomotion) that I immediately knew his intellectual grasp had deteriorated? Moreover, after I had greeted him he said: 'How's the Poet Laureate?' At once I realized that though he almost certainly knew who I was, he had read of my being voted to the Oxford Chair (which at the time had gained media publicity through there being a number of *outré* candidates, including the Soviet poet Yevtushenko), and momentarily imagined I had succeeded to the Laureateship, the question being rhetorical. The mistake was less venal than may be imagined, for Bonamy and I both knew the Poet Laureate, who in fact lived in adjacent Greenwich. I played along with his error, saying that as far as I knew the Laureate was all right. The enquiry had further plausibility, for at that time C. Day Lewis's final period of illnesses had already begun.

It must have been two years or so after this encounter that Georgina spoke to me on the telephone. The year was 1974; Valentine was dead. Georgina lived in north London, could not see her father as much as she would have liked, and he, now more or less house-bound, lacked people he could talk to. I said I would visit him, and so I did, I suppose about half a dozen times. I used to walk across the heath mid-morning to the house in Pond Road, where Bonamy would be lying, fully dressed, on a bed downstairs. On an early visit I encountered one of his neighbours on a similar mission: she told me that sometimes Bonamy had called on them in the middle of the night, oblivious of the unsuitability of the hour, difficult to get rid of. But I found him by no means completely gaga; rather, in the state of Act V Lear – though the book by his bedside was the Everyman volume of Shakespeare's *Comedies*, a choice that greatly impressed me, bringing to mind Yeats's 'Hamlet and Lear are gay; Gaiety transfiguring all that dread.' He was being looked after by a lady evidently used to such a task, competent and well-meaning, though conversing with him as though he were a child or simpleton, in the usual manner of nurses or para-nurses, and therefore getting far less response than if she had behaved to him normally. As in the old days, he offered me sherry: I was somewhat appalled when she diluted his glass with water, remarking only fairly *sotto voce* on her action. Whether or not he knew what was going on, he made no comment, pursuing what seemed to be his strategy of treating the nurse-housekeeper as though she did not exist, or at any rate had no real role to play in his affairs.

No doubt in our conversational exchanges I made a greater effort to amuse him than on the South Bank terrace years before. More than once on these visits he asked: 'How old am I?' I told him he was eighty-three: it so happened that I'd looked up his date of birth in *Who's Who*. He was still a handsome – even beautiful – man, the hair remaining shining silver, matching the military moustache. He sometimes mentioned Valentine. He knew she was dead, but referred to her rather as though she had gone unaccountably into some permanent exile, yet physically not utterly remote. His current life was without interest to him, so I tried to open up his memory by asking about his literary past, which stretched back to the years just after the First World War, when he contributed to the *London Mercury* and *New Statesman*, and brought out his book on Restoration Comedy. He talked about 'Tom' (T. S. Eliot) and 'Herbert' (Read), but his recollection of interesting detail was absent. The occasion reminded me of two radio interviews I had once conducted with Arthur Waley, when getting out of him early – any! – memories of Pound and Eliot was like the proverbial blood from a stone.

At the time of these visits I was writing the poems in triplets that now appear in Part 8 of *New and Collected Poems 1934–84*: included is the memorial poem for Bonamy, 'Last Dreams', which takes up some of the foregoing themes, and shows how deep was his last impression on me:

> Sagacious Ella Freeman Sharpe says dreams
> Are typical of the human mind and adds:
> 'The only dreamless state is death.' I note
>
> The place. Again some pages later: 'Our
> Essential life knows no mortality.'
> The obvious poignard strikes home to the heart.

When I release the walnuts' brainy shells
The husks' insides are as vein-netted as
Our human embryos. And gardening late

(The robin's song like snapping twigs or garden
Chairs being shut, the low sky jaundiced through
The trees), I see such things' nobility.

Each species has its general character –
The dunnock's patient pecking, say, at nothing;
Or human dreams – that conquers special marks.

The father, in the manner of all fathers
Once brushed the daughter's hair. Time has reversed
The roles. To mark my visit, silver silk

Above the mortal face. I wish I'd said:
'How beautiful you look!' Now it's too late.
In any case, would you have deigned to care?

In those last weeks we used to talk of Tom
And Herbert, best remembered of your friends:
Demotic names, high poets. Gone before you.

'How old am I?' you questioned more than once.
'You're eighty-three,' I said. 'I looked you up.'
You liked it not those months without your wife.

Your life at last seemed almost wholly dreams.
I chose for your committal lines those friends
Would have been sad though scarcely shocked to find

Apt for the grim but not ignoble rite:
'From an island of calm a limpid source of love.'
And 'Old men ought to be explorers.' It's

The final folding of the summer chair
The robin mimics. Now you can never know
The meaning of the strange recurring dream

In each man's life – one's reason to believe
It's always about some move into a great
And ruined house. Or have you fathomed it?

One day Georgina telephoned me to say that Bonamy had died; it was not long after my last visit. I do not know what the death certificate named as the cause of death: to me, as I put it in the poem, it seemed a case of the famous epitaph by Sir Henry Wotton. I thought *The Times* ought to be told of his death, not sure whether Georgina was going to announce it in the 'Births, Marriages and Deaths' columns. When I telephoned the Obituaries Department they seemed unacquainted with the name; in any case wanted to check with a relative. It was an insight into the risk of dying in old age, unnoticed by a world that had passed on, easily envisaged for oneself.

I travelled to the crematorium with Georgina and Valerie Eliot. Georgina had rigorously carried out what undoubtedly was Bonamy's wish – no religious ceremony – and had asked me to read something suitable. I thought the undertakers coped well with the unusual absence of a clergyman (a suitable firm for one's own obsequies), and they (or perhaps the verger) showed me two buttons by the lectern which I was to use in the right order when I had finished my reading: they were labelled MUSIC and INTERMENT. I had chosen two quite short passages from poems by Herbert and Tom. It was easy to find appropriate lines in Eliot – the last paragraph of 'East Coker', which turned out in the context to be extremely affecting, to the reader at least. Read proved a tougher nut to crack. I possessed his *Collected Poems*, knew them fairly well, but looking through the book for something that would strike home, however obliquely, I realized what a withdrawn and tenuous poet he was, matching his personality which, long before, I had awkwardly encountered once or twice at parties. When in due course I came to know his son, the novelist Piers Paul Read, though I was slightly taken aback at his saying that he did not care for his father's verse, on reflection I very well understood such a view. This is what I read, perhaps in the end not inappositely:

> Vision itself is desperate: the act
> Is born of the ideal: the hand
> Must seize the hovering grail.

The sense of glory stirs the heart
Out of its stillness: a white light
Is in the hills and the thin cry
Of a hunter's horn. We shall act
We shall build
A crystal city in the age of peace
Setting out from an island of calm
A limpid source of love.

Whether the mourners in the crematorium chapel (mainly Bonamy's and Valentine's local friends) made anything of the words at first hearing, may be doubted.

2

Like Bonamy, Sir George Rostrevor Hamilton had moved to Blackheath on his retirement. His knighthood had come through his distinction as a civil servant. Though he had a First in Greats from Oxford, he started humbly in the Inland Revenue at Somerset House, ending eventually (after being plucked from the ranks for a series of special posts) as Presiding Special Commissioner of Income Tax. But, as he said in the prefatory note to his *Collected Poems and Epigrams*, he 'never regarded poetry as a second string to that honourable profession [of civil servant], or as a hobby'. The volume of 1958 contains 356 pages but even so omits a large part of his previous work. A further collection, *Landscape of the Mind*, appeared in 1963.

The Hamiltons knew the Dobrées, but they are not associated in my mind as being together in physical space or in anything else. George and Marion were the children of clergymen and remained Christians, with conservative views and a high regard for decent and proper conduct. I am sure Bloomsbury seemed to them on the whole a raffish lot, and the leftwards swing of intellectual society in the Thirties was without effect on them. George's literary forebears could be said to be the Georgian poets – Walter de la Mare had been a valued friend. Other friends had been J. C. Squire, and Alice and Wilfrid Meynell and their family. Indeed, the Hamiltons stood for a whole literary ancestry, albeit a minor and quite out-of-fashion branch. For example, in their drawing-room I met Francis Meynell, son of the poet, founder of the Nonesuch Press, and Lady Noyes, widow of Sir Alfred. Alfred Noyes was the author of a poem, most of which I can still recite, in an anthology I 'did' for the Oxford Junior Local examination as a boy of fourteen:

> The moon is up: the stars are bright:
>   The wind is fresh and free!
> We're out to seek for gold to-night
>   Across the silver sea! . . .
>
> We're sick of all the cringing knees,
>   The courtly smiles and lies!
> God, let Thy singing Channel breeze
>   Lighten our hearts and eyes!

Thus it goes on. George Rostrevor Hamilton's poetry is in a less antiquated mode, but the Eliot–Pound revolution had passed him by. Or, rather, he had taken no account of it: his criticism proves him to have read widely, and a once, justly, famous essay called 'The Tell-Tale Article' had some acute words about modernist poetic diction. He was fortunate in his publisher. When George was a young man William Heinemann took a great fancy to his verse, and the firm, through all its changes of personnel, stayed loyal to him, so that he was spared the lowering searches for a publisher forced on many of us aged and unfashionable poets.

I must surely have first known George through a curious institution called 'The English Festival of Spoken Poetry'. It was held every year, mainly to confer awards for verse-speaking, but with a few ancillary events that concerned poetry in general. The organizers were on the alert to recruit younger poets as judges (not long after I started so serving I was joined by a girlish Elizabeth Jennings). Older hands included L. A. G. Strong and Richard Church, names to conjure with in their day, now perhaps forgotten (though in the Looking-glass world of modern Eng Lit the latter may live on in his role as a director of Dylan Thomas's publishers, J. M. Dent and Sons; in his

Letters the ineffable poet describing the kindly and gentle *littérateur* as 'a cliché-riddled humbug and pie-fingering hack'). I daresay I was flattered to be asked to figure in such a galaxy (also, I have been afflicted all my life by the kind of conscientiousness apt to lead to boring or uncongenial activities, then to be made the best of), but the thing was really not my cup of tea. After a few years, however, the competitive verse-speaking was dropped, and the occasion became simply a 'Festival of Poetry', later 'Poetry International', when native bards were joined by such as Allen Ginsberg, Ungaretti, and Hans Magnus Enzensberger – though I doubt if the proceedings engaged me much more. The first time I ever saw in the flesh my idol of the Thirties, W. H. Auden, was when at a Poetry International recital on the South Bank (very likely the same auditorium where Dame Edith sleep-walked) he came on the platform in a shabby brown suit. It must have been a very early (perhaps the first) public appearance of his in this country since his pre-war exile, and the audience, as moved as I was, accorded him remarkably prolonged applause.

Eventually we saw more of the Hamiltons than the Dobrées. This may have been because of Valentine's illness, though on the whole George and Marion offered much the easier social intercourse. They lived at first in a flat on the ground floor of Paragon House, a Georgian house at the corner of the heath and Pond Road, forming the end of a fine Georgian crescent known as the Paragon. Later they moved to a rather more spacious flat in the Paragon itself. Over the years they had accumulated some choice furniture, paintings and books: nothing extravagantly valuable, merely what could have been afforded out of a discriminating civil servant's salary. There especially springs to mind a fine collection of Nonesuch Press books, and a painting bought from Victor Pasmore when they were neighbours of his in their previous house in Chiswick Mall. It may have been pure coincidence that in Blackheath they were still neighbours, for Victor and his wife had for some time owned a house on the east side of the heath. The painting in question was in Victor's attractive Impressionist style: the intervening years had diverted him wholly to Abstraction.

The Pasmores were only two of a good few we first met, or renewed acquaintance with, round the Hamiltons' dining-table. The process continued after George's death: Marion liked me to do the drinks, and open and serve the wine, though neither she nor I attempted to concoct the cocktail that George had invariably mixed and offered his guests, a brew whose ingredients I never discovered and always avoided. Except for puddings, Marion was not a *cordon bleu*, but she took a great deal of trouble, and the guests, even after she was left a widow, were usually of interest – for instance, Burke Trend, when he was Secretary to the Cabinet, and ever at the risk of being called to Downing Street, even after the dinner-party was over. She was a strong woman, in mind and body (despite a chronic internal affliction), indefatigable in theatre- and concert-going, especially devoted to opera. George, I should say, was practically tone-deaf, but nobly tagged along on these musical occasions. Each was the great love of the other's life.

When we became friends with the Hamiltons I knew his name as a poet, but had scarcely read his work. In earlier days I was a stern – even rude – reviewer of verse. I expect I should have been stern, though probably not rude, about George's. At one time I would have condemned out of hand those poets who had not accepted the challenge of Eliot/Pound, and the American poets of the inter-war years, and the Auden generation. I did not lose this over-devotion to the *zeitgeist* until quite late in life, and thus for a long time was partially blind to the virtues of a poet like Ruth Pitter. Fortunately I had never had to review George, for I doubt I should have found much in his favour – though I liked the poem of his I knew best, the four-line epigram in, of all places, Auden's and Garrett's anthology, *The Poet's Tongue*:

Don's Holiday

Professor Robinson each summer beats
The fishing record of the world – such feats
As one would hardly credit from a lesser
Person than a history professor.

But when *Landscape of the Mind* came out I thought it marked a fresh turn to his verse, and agreed to review it for the *London Magazine*. The editor, then Alan Ross, probably had a soft spot for George on account of his elegiac 'Ode to a Cricketer: W. G. Quaife', otherwise I doubt if a notice would have appeared in such an *avant garde* place. A couple of years later George published a book I admired still more (indeed, in its way a forgotten minor classic) – the autobiographical *Rapids of Time*. It reveals a transparently good and innocent man, which he was. I remember him saying he did not know the meaning of the word 'condom' (now bandied about by babes and sucklings), which I had used in a poem, but fortunately some diversion spared my giving a definition. This is a trivial, even ambiguous, indication of character, yet it has stuck with me as touchingly typical.

One of the earliest indications of George's failing powers occurred when he and Marion were greeting us on a visit to their Paragon flat. Men and women had exchanged kisses – probably the women, too, and then as the final act of the sequence George implanted a kiss on *my* cheek. He was at once embarrassed, far more than I – though in Victorian times the osculation would have gone unmarked: Alfred Lyttelton records Ruskin giving a tender kiss of greeting to Carlyle (received 'kindly enough'). Two subsequent instances come vividly to mind. Ensconced in the corner of a settee in our sitting-room, George stretched out a leg (he was a tall man) into the settee's vacant space. It was a gesture to be thought nothing of, but Marion was horrified, and ordered the offending limb down. On a later occasion, at our dining-table, George utterly uncharacteristically used his fingers to convey to himself some morsel of food. If Marion saw this, she refrained from comment: it may be by then such lapses were more common. I remember thinking that the action was a regression to childhood days.

Apropos of George's decline, Marion said that in her experience it was the keenest brains that were most liable to decay. George's amiability, good manners even, tended to make one forget he had written a book on Bergson and philosophy (subtitled 'An Essay on the Scope of Intelligence'), and indeed that in his final year at Oxford he had been as good as offered (and rejected) a Fellowship at his college. His chapter on Bergson, brief though it is, has abiding interest. On one of his visits to Bergson in Paris, he one day found with him 'a studious-looking bearded figure' who proved to be none other than Lorentz, whom Einstein had called the greatest man, the most powerful thinker he had known.

It was not long before George deteriorated physically as well as mentally, but we did not see him at that time. One day, during our stay at Torquay for a Building Societies Association conference, I opened *The Times* and with sadness saw his obituary. It was ample and, I think, judicious. It surprised Marion, she told us later, by its amplitude. It did not surprise me, since I was the author: writing it had been a rather grisly duty of a few years before, alleviated by the sense that I was doing justice to a man who had never written (and probably never uttered) an unworthy word. I wonder if Marion guessed the authorship: I have the feeling she did, but she never let on.

Marion lived a courageous widowhood, by no means slowing up on entertaining, holidays abroad, listening to music. She seemed indestructible (even her hair never lost its brown) but of course in the end she had to re-join George – and I am sure she believed it would be in a mode superior to common mortality. One evening when we had dined with her she asked me if I would like to have George's OED. It was the thirteen volumes of the original edition, each volume (except possibly the last supplementary and miscellaneous one) requiring a feat of strength to consult (in fact, when Logan Pearsall Smith needed to consult them in old age he used to call in the young Robert Gathorne Hardy to lug them about). Somehow the volumes seemed even heavier through having had to endure a flooding by the Thames when they reposed in the Hamiltons' house in Chiswick Mall that had formerly belonged to J. C. Squire. It was a gift of unlimited potential. Some time after Marion's death, in a secondhand bookshop in Blackheath Village, I saw the slender india-paper edition of Robert Bridges's *The Spirit of Man*, a book I quite wished to possess. When I opened it, I found Marion's bold signature on the inside cover, with the date, 1920. She had then been a bride of two years. I bought the anthology and, with conscious sentiment, added my own name, and the date – 28 November 1979.

<h2 style="text-align:center">3</h2>

I had no clear critical sheet in respect of two other poets who came to live in Blackheath after the war. *Twentieth Century Verse* was a little magazine of the Thirties: through my contributing to it had come my friendship with its editor, Julian Symons. In its December 1938 issue I had reviewed C. Day Lewis's new book of poems, *Overtures to Death*. After a first paragraph of rather schoolmasterish analysis of its contents, I went on to write the following. (It should be explained that at that time Day Lewis was a convinced and active Marxist, a stance I wholeheartedly approved of: my words demonstrate how much I must have disliked the actual poems.)

> Most of the virtue belonging to conviction and activity is cancelled out by the extraordinary way in which these poems are written. Sleep has night-scented borders, the night a grave manifold of stars, smoke rolls forth, the week is russet and rejoicing, elms toss their heads and are spring-garlanded, three cloud-maidens rise wind-flushed . . . Mr D. L. has now lost the knack, which even a minor poet with sufficient ambition and application may acquire, of writing verse one might care to re-read. There are too many poems here which could have been improved by ten minutes' work, too many which are merely lazy literary responses to questions which (to Mr D. L.'s credit) are posed to all of us. His talent is not so lovely that it can afford to go about ungroomed, even on party business.

Did Cecil ever see this? If so, it would have stuck in his memory, for he was affected by bad notices. After the war I came across him a few times on various literary chores, but there was nothing untoward in those meetings. By then he was a distinguished literary figure, and his authorship of the successful 'Nicholas Blake' crime novels was widely known. He was an extremely good-looking man, always well-dressed in a faintly horsy style (raglan overcoats, small-checked suits). At first an austere manner was conveyed, appropriate to encountering a whipper-snapper who had once impudently reviewed him; but eventually the features would break into a smile, and he would prove himself to be someone who liked a joke, not averse to telling one at his own expense.

At the end of 1957 he came to live, with his second wife (Jill Balcon, the actress) and two children by her, in a Georgian house at the bottom of Croom's Hill, a road that runs from Blackheath heath down to Greenwich, containing a conspectus of British domestic architecture from the middle of the seventeenth century onwards. It was a few years before we began to exchange visits, I think first getting to know one another better round the Hamiltons' dining-table. Jill proved to have a great talent for entertaining and being entertained, and her personality prompted Cecil the more easily to let his hair down. No doubt there lurked always in his manner his sense of being a great man – not that he was in any way affected or pretentious; more that a feeling of his being on the *qui vive* was conveyed, against what precisely rather difficult to define. It is somewhat extraordinary that when one comes to give an account of him, personality and anecdotal memories are thin on the ground. Somewhere in his autobiography he says how much he hated large parties, and it may well have been that despite his success with women and in public appearances as verse reader, he was basically shy, a quality easily mistaken for other qualities, not always endearing. (After she had read this account of Cecil, Jill rightly referred me to his poem 'Almost Human', in which he mercilessly delineates the contradictions of a poet's occupation and character – the 'outlaw and cripple' under the 'valued skin'; the 'cold, strange heart' that nevertheless tries to share the common human tragedies for which the poet finds 'immortal phrases'.)

When I read his son's posthumous biography (a fascinating though sometimes startlingly unfilial book) I was surprised to find that in 1960 Cecil (who was on the relevant committee) had advanced my claim (though in vain) to a Queen's Gold Medal for Poetry. If he had ever known of my review of *Overtures to*

Death he had magnanimously put it out of mind, nor was it as though by 1960 I knew him really well. When we started to go to Croom's Hill, his children by Jill, Tamasin and Daniel, were out of infancy, both showing the striking looks that contributed to Daniel following his mother into the world of the theatre. Sometimes a, to me, legendary figure would be a fellow dinner guest: I would instance John Garrett, the joint editor, with Auden, of *The Poet's Tongue*, already mentioned – influential anthology of 1935 (which followed Bridges's *The Spirit of Man* in withholding the poets' names beside the poems) whose Introduction was a sacred text of my youth; and Alec Brown, who to the Spring 1936 number of *New Writing* contributed an English version of Pasternak's '1905'. I should emphasize again that though I followed closely the Thirties movement in literature, it was mainly from afar. And when I say 'closely', I wonder if I really read through, and with any critical insight, Alec Brown's Pasternak translation – which, having taken down from the shelf the dusty and foxed relevant issue of *New Writing*, I now find skilful and effective:

> Think; in our time; and turned to a lecturer's catchword;
> and the fettering years since then have made such a clatter
> the whole damn thing is forgotten, and all that occurred
> is no legend inspiring, but a frigid 'historical' matter . . .

I expect, if I read the version at all attentively in the spring of 1936, I would have been interested in its 'revolutionary' content and how to bring such matters into verse, rather than its 'poetic' qualities and its usage of the characteristic tone of native English verse. And as to Thirties political beliefs, Cecil once expressed surprise (and, I think, a touch of sympathetic fellow feeling) that I had been then, like him, for a short time a member of the Communist Party.

The last years of Cecil's life were marked by a number of illnesses, all of which he treated with stoicism, even levity. After a bladder-stones operation he kept the offending minerals on the mantelpiece of his study, part of the relics on show there, which included a framed holograph poem by Wilfred Owen. This room, at the front of the ground-floor, with stripped

panelling and many bookshelves, was as elegant as its inhabi-
tant. On my first entering it I had observed twin, floor-standing
loud-speakers of discriminating make, so when I called after
one of his hospitalizations (perhaps the stones removal) I
brought as a gift the duplicate of a disc, cheap, but which had
given me great pleasure. It was a realization of Bach's 'Musical
Offering' by a Czech ensemble, which made of that somewhat
enigmatic piece a work of inexhaustible interest. I liked to think
it helped Cecil to get shot of a poem or two – a process which
involved also the smoking of many cigarettes, as Jill once told
me.

By consulting a pocket diary of engagements I find I last saw
Cecil on 20 January 1972. The occasion was a sort of business
lunch at *L'Escargot* restaurant in Soho to which he and I had
been invited by Jack Clark, old friend of mine who had become
the brother-in-law of Julian Symons. Jack, and his partner in a
firm of advertising agents, had conceived and carried into effect
an enterprise called 'Poem of the Month Club'. The notion was
that subscribers would receive every month a new poem,
specially printed, and signed by the author. To confer prestige
on what was designed to be a non-loss-making venture, the
selectors were the Poet Laureate and the Oxford Professor of
Poetry, offices held by Cecil and me respectively. At *L'Escargot*
it seemed plain that Cecil had cancer: he had lost weight, said he
couldn't keep warm. But he attributed his illness to diabetes,
which symptom-wise may have been correct, for he had an
inoperable tumour on the pancreas. He was forbidden wine,
opened capsules and sprinkled the powder on his food, implied
it might not go down at all well. His hands seemed to be taking
on a transparency. But he was not in the least sorry for himself,
and indeed had to leave for some other engagement while Jack
and I were still at table. I saw him being helped on with his
overcoat by a waiter, an office he seemed really to require, by no
means a mere restaurant courtesy. I often thought of him with
compassion thereafter, thinking of the suffering of both my
parents from his disease.

Cecil died on the 22 May. At quite short notice I was asked
by Alan Haydock, a BBC radio producer I had worked with

before, to compile and read a memorial programme of Cecil's poems. It was broadcast on 24 May. Looking through Cecil's poetry for this occasion, I saw clearly that his talent had survived Auden's overpowering influence, the crude political demands of the Thirties, and his own tendency to lapse into the received 'poetic' (it must be remembered he was born in 1904, passed his adolescence in a time when the Georgian poets – and worse – were still influential). Rehearsing and recording the poems I had chosen, I realized how well they were laid out for the voice (he was an excellent reader of verse), even the complex stanza-forms, and how observing the metrics made plainer the sense. The experience touched me: I felt things had moved on for the better since that rude review nearly thirty-four years before.

4

Virtually at the top of Croom's Hill, within the curtilege of Greenwich Park, a fine old house, Macartney House, had long been converted into flats. One of them had once been occupied by the Woolwich executive Sandy Meikle: into another, or possibly the same one, had come John Pudney and his second wife, Monica. He was a poet I had known about ever since his first book had been scathingly reviewed in the February 1934 number of *New Verse* by Geoffrey Grigson, that little magazine's editor. Pudney had been in the Royal Air Force during the war, and, though starting out as a minority poet, his wartime verse had caught the imagination of a wider public, two short poems actually being quoted in a famous film of the period, *The Way to the Stars*, as though the work of the RAF character played by Michael Redgrave. The better-known was called 'Airman' and began:

> Fetch out no shroud
> For Johnny-in-the-cloud;
> And keep your tears
> For him in after years.

I, too, had written poetry while in the Forces during the war; no doubt had a pang or two of envy at John Pudney's popularity (the sales of his wartime work were said by his publishers in 1948 to have exceeded 100,000 copies).

In 1948 I reviewed a new collection of his for the left-wing weekly, *Tribune*. I was very severe with it, and, what was quite unfair, mocked his popularity, asserting he was now not so much a poet as a phenomenon, having 'taken a place in the glass-fronted bookcase beside Omar Khayyam and Rupert Brooke'. In next week's *Tribune* a letter to the editor from the poet appeared, which began:

> The rather silly views of Mr Roy Fuller upon Recent Poetry [the heading of the notice] are of no particular consequence in themselves. He is evidently a person who must first express a measure of bile before facing his own problems in literature.
>
> What surprises me, sir, is that your journal, which at one time seemed to be concerned with the propagation of thought and culture among the rank-and-file of the country, should encourage this person to sneer at the fact that my former volumes reached a wide public . . .

The editor appended a note about the freedom of opinion of his contributors, but it must be admitted John Pudney had made an effective point. This exchange was very much in my mind when I was due to meet the poet and his wife at the Hamiltons', perhaps twenty years after. But the encounter passed off unremarkably: neither of us disinterred the past. I expect I silently confirmed on that occasion that John abstained from any alcoholic drink. He had made no secret of his former addiction; indeed, it formed the subject of some of his occasional journalism. Drink had perhaps contributed to the break-up of his first marriage to the daughter of the once celebrated author and MP, A. P. Herbert. His second wife, Monica – intelligent and agreeable – seemed devoted to him, and one guessed she had played no small part in his conquest of the Demon Drink. John had gone on writing verse, but since he lived by his pen was also the author of many miscellaneous books and much journalism.

I went to a party the Pudneys gave at Macartney House; perhaps came across them on other occasions, but I never got to know John at all closely. He was only three years older than me; we could have had a good deal in common, but in person he has left little more impression than a middle-aged individual of medium height and average looks. What stays in my mind is his enviable courage. I don't know how I heard he had contracted cancer of the throat: it may well have been that he turned the disaster to journalistic account, as he had his alcoholism. The malady was possibly a legacy of his drinking past, but that would not have made it any easier to come to terms with. It was after he had undergone surgery that he, Monica and I attended a tree-planting ceremony in Greenwich Park. Could it have been in 1977 to mark the Silver Jubilee of the Queen's accession? The reason for two poets being invited also eludes me. The episode is one of many become mysterious in the recollection of old age. But I remember feeling, that bright, sharp morning, as we met, like conferring monarchs, from our opposite sides of the Park, a greater intimacy with him than before. Probably the faintly lunatic proceedings, and certainly one's concerned enquiries about his health, brought us closer; and Monica's presence was always a catalyst. George Rostrevor Hamilton had loved to walk on the heath, Cecil Day Lewis in the Park – both had written poems about their peregrinations – but John and I seemed the last of the Blackheath poets. (In the Eighties a young poet, Blake Morrison, came to live in the Pudneys' old flat, but that is another story, as must remain the recent Blackheath presence of yet another poet, Herbert Lomas.) John was optimistic about his health, and in fact his looks and demeanour seemed to justify optimism. But eventually I read a newspaper article by him, characteristically forthcoming and gay, in which he recounted his inability to swallow, and his being fed direct into (I think) the oesophagus. His words were intended to reassure – perhaps did reassure – fellow sufferers, but they upset me, evidence of one further step into the inevitable pit.

After his death Monica asked me to join with several other poets (including Bertie Lomas) in a memorial reading for her husband, held in the Ranger's House, another fine old house, near Macartney House, on the edge of the Park. We could choose the poems we wished to read, Monica even supplying typescripts of uncollected, perhaps unpublished, poems. The choice was more difficult than had been the case with Cecil's commemorative programme. Quite strange, the itch to associate oneself only with what one is capable of defending – a sort of snobbery. But as I looked through John's work, I saw that he was best as a writer of light, even comic, verse – subsequently proved by the reactions of a live audience. I was obtuse not to have seen that in 1948, and thus been able to express sympathy in my review instead of contumely.

5

I feel confident that I met another Blackheath poet through none of the foregoing channels. The agency may well have been the Blackheath Poetry Society, a stubbornly flourishing organization I read my verse to on a couple of occasions, and whose annual garden parties in the Barnards' beautiful garden in Pond Road I still attend. When I first got to know her, Patricia Ledward had come to live at the other end of the road in which we also then lived, St John's Park; a slim, pale girl, not long married to Walter Simon. Her maiden name had been familiar to me certainly since 1943, when she appeared in an anthology called *More Poems from the Forces* edited by Keidrych Rhys, himself a name known pre-war through Julian Symons. During the war she had been in the ATS, a driver with an anti-aircraft unit. Some have seen merit in my depiction of the unparalleled boredom of service life: Patricia's best-known poem, 'Evening in Camp', does this all the more touchingly with a female cast:

> To weary senses all things are
> The tone of khaki, hair and eyes and skin,
> And girls relaxed on chairs and floor are still
> With the stillness of saints;
> The light is dim and voices
> So slow it seems they dream.

> At this hour of quietness we wonder:
> Where are we? What are we doing?
> Perhaps we are players in a Russian scene,
> Crouching around the stove discussing
> Love and death and the dusty path of time . . .

Did the Muse give her the go-by with the coming of peace? It may have been so, for when we got to know her she was publishing prose, notably a *roman à thèse* about the ardours of twin boys arriving additionally to a not very old baby daughter. Patricia was the daughter of the sculptor Gilbert Ledward, whom I met on several occasions when the Simons had moved to a house whose back garden fronted the lane to which we had moved. Gilbert and I found common ground not only in Kenya, where I had been during the war, and which he had visited for material for a Commonwealth war memorial, but also the Blackpool cenotaph of the First World War, which he had designed and whose unveiling in the Twenties I had actually attended with a party from school. He was a humorous, ironic man I took to at once, and Patricia, sensing this, invited me after his death to choose a drawing by him as a memento. I selected, aptly enough, a sheet of studies of the nude black male, presumably for the memorial before mentioned.

In 1986 I wrote a poem about this drawing:

21. XII. 86

> 'The sun is furthest south at 4. 02
> Tomorrow morning.' Thus the *Sunday Times*.
> Quite soon I shall be waking in the light,
> Or resting after lunch without the sun
> Bothering my sight, and fading on the wall
> The study, pale enough, that Ledward made
> For some memorial to the Empire's slain.

> Old Gilbert, gone himself these umpteen years:
> Who now remembers him, even passing his work?
> Fortunate sun, to come back from the dead –

So might be thought; yet, calculating one's
Chances of seeing the other solstice, it
Must strike home that there's something to be said
For war-free slumbering, *oeuvre* cast in bronze.

I sent Patricia a copy of the periodical in which this first appeared. It drew from her a communication which began: 'Old Gilbert's name isn't altogether forgotten, dear Roy. For instance, the monetary value of his work is gradually rising. For instance, in an exhibition last year his "Monolith" was rescued from the Tate, dusted down and attracted a lot of interest. For instance, the Fine Art Society is celebrating his centenary this year with a small exhibition of drawings that trace his career – more or less. Phew – I grow breathless in my re-animation of Papa's reputation!' I was duly chastened; went to the centenary exhibition. Gilbert's draughtsmanship shone out all the more brightly in an era by and large of rotten drawing.

Patricia's life had its share of sorrows, and years before this she had moved to Brighton, whether retaining any literary ambitions I do not know, though as demonstrated, we kept some kind of contact. In 1984 I went to a reception and reading at the Imperial War Museum to mark the publication of Catherine Reilly's anthology of women's poetry of the Second World War, in which Patricia's work was represented. The occasion moved me to a poem, which ends with me reading the anthology

                    plonk-softened, in
The bus that takes me home along the once
Bomb-fractured Old Kent Road, and so return
The names and phrases half-forgotten since
My wartime years. I think what myriad
Lovers and chums and verse those years threw up;
Perverse as ever, showings of the human.
Great girls, who wept for England and for us;
Meriting more than blank pentameters –
Muted Elgarian trombones at least.

6

So, while others declined and passed away, I was spared to become, so I hope, a better poet, certainly to write a good deal of poetry. Julian Symons was spared with me (we were both born in 1912) but he eventually deserted Blackheath and, to a great degree, the writing of verse. Jill Day Lewis and Monica Pudney also moved elsewhere. But I will not end on a note of change and decay. A book of poems I published in 1954, *Counterparts*, includes a poem with the dedication 'JLF, his poem'. It had been written during a family holiday in 1952 on the Côte des Maures, and the dedication acknowledges my son's contribution to most of the imagery at the start of the poem:

> The azure marbled with white and palest grey:
> The cactuses with buds like hand grenades:
> The roman candle palms: a lonely house
> Against a hill, a wrong piece of a jig-saw.
> The terraces descend in armour plating,
> The grapes a violet shadow in their vines.

John was then only fifteen, but I suppose I must have guessed he was going to join the number of the Blackheath poets.

III

WITH THE WOOLWICH

I

As PREVIOUSLY stated, I returned to the Woolwich in 1946. Later that year Alexander Meikle became its sole General Manager. Since 1943 he had held the office jointly with Austin E. Smith, but the latter had become ill, and he resigned from the Society's service not awfully long after my return. His illness was rumoured to be tuberculosis; never made wholly unambiguous, at least to a relative underling like myself. It was also said that Sandy Meikle had manoeuvred Austin into premature retirement, his ancient ambition being to succeed to an unshared General Managership. It seemed to me then, rather more certainly than it seems to me now, that this was so. The two men were much of an age; at any rate, Austin was young enough to ensure that given good health his joint tenure would last a good few years. Sandy's ambition had undoubtedly been sharpened by the shape the Society's organization took during the war years.

The Munich crisis of 1938 had prompted the Society – theoretically especially vulnerable to German air-attack in south-east London – to seek country premises where its accounts and securities (and a proportion of its staff) would be safe on the outbreak of hostilities. A large house, with out-buildings, that had been used as a school, was found on the downs above Westerham in Kent, convenient in a way to Woolwich. It was on the ancient route of the Canterbury pilgrims, and had been named Pilgrim House. One of my early tasks on first appointment was to carry out the conveyancing of the property to the Society. They constructed a tunnel in the downs, lined it with shelving, and when war came transferred to it the thousands of

45

bundles of deeds of properties in mortgage to the Society. The
accounting departments, with their machines, were also transferred, so that amoeba-like, the Society had divided itself into
two. As Assistant Secretary, the senior executive on that side of
the business, Sandy was put in charge of the Westerham
offshoot, an assignment he enormously relished. All its wartime
activities became legendary in his telling of them, a process
assisted by his capacious memory, and his gift of the gab both in
private and public. Indeed, his gifts of various kinds were as
great as any I encountered, though in the end my acquaintance
ranged among the highest in the land, as they say. He could
have managed any large-scale enterprise, or been a sought-after
counsel or solicitor (he rapidly grasped the abstrusest legal
point, and had a love of so doing). In later days, when I felt I
could let my hair down with him, I once told him he would have
made a good lawyer. I could see he was pleased. His management of men was ruthless: some might have seen this as a fault,
but in my view staff should always feel happier when the
manager is, for some reason, absent from among them (I may
say I failed to carry this out when I became head of my
department). On the other hand (and this I found out only
when, succeeding Fred Shrimpton as the Society's solicitor, I
had to work closely with Sandy), if any member of staff was in
ill-health or otherwise fallen on evil days, there was nothing he
would not do for him or her, usually by stealth. I myself got on
well with him: I used to say to Kate that to do this you had to
stand up to him, but this was not a sure-fire *modus vivendi*, as
the case of John Lindsay illustrates.

Jack (as I followed his wife in calling him, though known in
the office as John) had been recruited to the Society towards the
end of the war, when I had been absent on war service. Like
Sandy (and several other of the Society's senior executives), he
was a Scottish accountant, a strain Sandy himself had introduced into the Woolwich. He also had a law degree, and before
the war had been with the Trustee Savings Bank, becoming
during the war a temporary, though quite senior, civil servant.
Sandy and Austin having been promoted joint General
Managers in 1943, the separate post of Secretary was created,

which Jack was to occupy. It was undoubtedly represented to him as an important appointment, with prospects of even more importance as the Society grew, which it was surely destined to do when peace returned, as it had in the past.

What went wrong? Jack was an ambitious man, and though not of Sandy's calibre, could have been guaranteed to undertake successfully any reasonable responsibility in the building society world. But in the post of Secretary his duties were narrowed down to serving the Board of Directors, which met fortnightly, and its not more frequent committees. Further power was denied him: moreover, in such responsibility as he had, Jack was subject to the unrelenting edge of Sandy's sharp side. Jack did not lack courage in facing these frustrations, but in the end came to see that the fulfilment of his ambitions would have to take place outside the Society. He was short-listed for at least one top executive's job with another society, but he had really hung on with the Woolwich too long in the hope of improving his scope, and as he moved towards retirement age he had to become enured to his relatively modest post.

He got on with members of the Board and served them well, lending a sympathetic ear to *their* frustrations, always prevalent among non-executive directors. He had a brainwave one day, and suggested reviving the Society's pre-war staff journal. I was asked to become its editor, on account of my literary side, which I suppose had become known to the Society through my two wartime books of verse, but Jack really ran the thing, enjoyed doing so. It was not wholly on account of our collaboration in this enterprise that we fell into the habit of going out for mid-morning coffee together: I had quickly grown to like him very much, and he loved to confide in me, not only about the progress of his war with Sandy, but also about his pre-Woolwich life. Our coffee venue was the Express Dairy next door (across the basement garage ramp) to Equitable House, the Society's imposing Thirties-built headquarters. There was a tinge of illegality, or at any rate (in fairly senior executives) eccentricity, in leaving Equitable House for mid-morning refreshment, for that could be obtained more easily from the staff restaurant on the top floor. And in fact, in 1958, when I succeeded Fred Shrimpton, I told Jack that I felt I ought to set a better example, and our sessions continued in my room or his. I say 'his', but in later days he lost his room (space in Equitable House becoming exiguous), and had to set up his desk in a large committee-room adjoining the Boardroom, which doubled as the senior executives' luncheon room. This was undoubtedly authorized, if not planned, by Sandy. I think for me it would have been the signal for a complete show-down, or departure at any price (though easy to say this), but Jack bore it well, really without loss of prestige.

His fatal ties with the Society were strengthened by ill-health, including the loss by surgery of gall-bladder and one kidney. From these misfortunes, though, he had recovered amazingly well (physically strong, as a young man only ill-luck – dogging him even then – had prevented him from being capped for Scotland's amateur soccer XI). He paid no attention to medical advice to avoid fatty delicacies like cream, which he loved as an adjunct to a very sweet tooth. So he came up to normal retirement at sixty-five. By that time I had retired prematurely as the Society's solicitor, and been elevated to the Board, in succession to Fred Shrimpton, who had thoughtfully made way for me. Post-war, the Board had been recruited (apart from Sandy and Fred) from national rather than local big-wigs, as appropriate to the Society's ever-increasing size. In my view, a disadvantage of this was that the directors tended to become in the eyes of the staff remote personae, making merely fleeting visits to Woolwich. I wrote an inspired letter to Sandy, pointing out the advantages of appointing Jack to the Board when he retired as Secretary – his quite near residence to Woolwich, his knowledge of the Society's affairs, particularly at Board level, and his undoubted ability to transform himself with dignity from executive to director. I suppose long odds might have been offered against this communication bearing fruit, but I had a curious sense of suddenly swimming with a changed tide. Sandy supported Jack's candidature, and he was duly elected. It was rather as though his retirement had been equivalent to his falling on evil days, and Sandy's Jekyll side had been activated.

One can only guess at the extent of Jack's pleasure. He had made many friends in the building societies world: his translation meant he would go on seeing them at conferences and so forth, and with increased prestige. His years of frustration were probably more than paid for. He assiduously attended Board and committee meetings, staff functions, prize-givings, and the like. Round the Board table he could often recall useful lessons from past meetings in the light of his long experience as the directors' servant. As a matter of fact, he had one thing in common with Sandy (apart from their nationality, profession, and prowess at golf) and that was their love of the Society. Despite his managerial ruthlessness, Sandy never forgot the principles that animated the founders of the building society 'movement' (now absurdly calling itself the 'industry'). The safety of the investors' cash (and its bearing sufficient interest to retain them) was obviously paramount, but borrowers were treated with as much leniency as was consonant with sensible management; in individual cases of disaster usually with generosity (the evil days principle again). The aim was not profit, for there were no equity shareholders, but a surplus sufficient to keep up the proper proportion of reserves and to enable the Society to expand within sound limits.

In 1969 Sandy became Chairman of the Board. It was, in a way, a Proustian transformation. He had only been elected to the Board after fifteen years of General Managership, in 1958 – the sole executive director among ten or so quite eminent men. It is true that his predecessor, T. R. Chandler, had eventually become Chairman, but he was a legendary figure even in his lifetime, having joined the Society in 1914, and seen it through its transmogrification from a local to a national enterprise. Moreover, on the very morning of the day he was due to preside for the first time at an annual general meeting, he collapsed and died. Sandy was given ample years to make his mark as Chairman, and subsequently (through his own voluntary resignation) as ordinary member. These final chapters of his career may have seemed inevitable to some, but to me who remembered him as the slim, young Assistant Secretary of 1938 before his Westerham avatar – the rise to the summit represented a manoeuvre of enormous skill and patience. Of course, at the end it was no great surprise: in fact, in Sandy's quite early days on the Board, Jack Lindsay had told me of Sandy's ambition, whether of divination or from the horse's mouth I am not sure. Probably the latter, for Sandy's oppression of Jack did not exclude an intimate intercourse between them – as with husband and wife at loggerheads.

Sandy did not quite die in harness. Out of the blue, diabetes was diagnosed. No scotch for him at the pre-Board luncheon drinks gathering. But it seemed a not too serious crack in the strong façade. He himself treated the business as something under his control (like appointments to the Society's staff or its annual surplus), as he did at a graver stage when lesions in his heels failed to heal, even after skin grafts. The adjuncts of his life had been chosen for reliability: he never used a cigarette lighter, always matches; never fountain pens, ballpoints or propelling pencils, always pen and ink, and pencils that had to be sharpened. But even dubious or inferior items he could bless into excellence through his use of them: 'perfect' he would pronounce an over-ambitious dish provided by the staff restaurant for the Board luncheon.

Then he underwent a double amputation, and had to resign from the Board. His wife, Peggy, had long been disabled, through a stroke, so Sandy wrecked up in a nursing-home, farther out into Kent even than his house, which since the Society's wartime division had been at Westerham; his last dwelling, a new house, christened by him with nostalgia 'Pilgrims'. I visited him in the nursing-home. It was a large, gloomy, main-road house, its institutionalized rooms and passages haunted depressingly by dim geriatrics. Sandy's brain, though, was as keen as ever, and he carried off, as surely one would have failed oneself to carry off, the travelling-rug that concealed the absence of his lower legs. He quite soon directed me to a bottle of Johnny Walker stowed away in his wardrobe, and joined me in a tot – undoubtedly feeling that no worse could befall by breaking his dietary regime. What the quality of life was for him in that time of survival I do not know: the thought of it was disturbing. Jack told me that on a visit by his wife

Rena, Sandy had said to her that he wondered if he had been right in consenting to his amputations, a speculation he would surely have only revealed to a woman, a category of humans he liked. Rena, who as a dentist was not without medical authority, and not one to mince her words, told him that if he hadn't he would be dead. But I suppose he never really recovered from the trauma of the surgery, and one couldn't but be thankful for him, in a way, to hear fairly soon of his end.

His physical presence removed from the world (as though in his days as General Manager he had gone on a vast holiday), the lesser men remaining felt able to add touches of levity to their anecdotes about him, though round the Board table Sandy's conjectured disapproval of some course of action for some time still carried weight. One story related by Douglas Carnegie, Sandy's chauffeur for many years, may stand for a good few, though it is somewhat extreme. One morning, when Douglas picked his master up to take him to the office, he was told by Sandy that in the evening, instead of driving him home, he was to drive him to a garage, where his own car would be ready for collection after servicing. At that time Sandy had moved to 'Pilgrims', which was on the downs on the far side of Westerham. In the evening, the utterly reliable Douglas, with Sandy aboard, coming to a crucial turning, continued so as to bring them to the garage. Sandy cried out: 'You're going the wrong way, you're going the wrong way.' Without doubt he thought that Douglas had forgotten the move to 'Pilgrims' and was taking him to his old house, as of yore. 'I thought you wanted to pick up your car,' said Douglas. 'Quite right,' Sandy replied, with complete aplomb. 'I was just testing you out.' One must add that Douglas related this with admiration.

2

My first substantial task on rejoining the Society had to do with Sandy's empire, Pilgrim House. The tunnel in the chalk that housed the deeds was, all too late, discovered to be damp. Many deeds and documents had begun to disintegrate. An electrical ventilating system was installed. One day, through it shorting, a fire was started among the deeds. By the time it was extinguished a fair number of bundles had been affected. One result was bizarre: deeds written on parchment shrank to perhaps a tenth of their size, dolls' house deeds, the back-sheets quite legible but the deed itself seized-up, unopenable. The title of the houseowner (and hence of the Society) had to be reconstituted in all cases where damage had caused the constituent documents to be illegible. Where the property was being sold or otherwise dealt with, reconstitution was urgent. Otherwise the work was of a plodding, on-going kind. The man who had been doing it until my return was a vastly experienced managing clerk whose employment by a City firm of solicitors on its litigation side had terminated because of the war. He had then been recruited by Fred Shrimpton to help plug the gaps left by the younger men of the solicitor's department who had disappeared on national service.

A good solicitor's managing clerk is capable of most tasks set before him, and the Society soon had its eye on Mr Cox. Not long after my return he was transferred to manage the Society's arrears department, a considerable promotion, with a scope I am sure never contemplated by him in pre-war days. He rose to the occasion, but left me with a hard core of damaged deeds cases – a score or so of bundles that had resisted reconstitution. The fire had occurred among the 'S's – dread initial as it came to be, even SMITH, my wife's maiden name, taking on unpleasant overtones. Reconstitution of title, in the Society's terms, consisted in no less than registering the borrower at the Land Registry with an absolute title. The Registry was accommodating, but even minimum requirements proved exasperatingly difficult to get hold of in this obdurate residue. Where the conveyance to the borrower had been burnt in the tunnel, the draft conveyance in his solicitor's possession had to be proved by statutory declaration; likewise the mortgage to the Society. Sometimes, in slipshod solicitors' offices, the drafts had never been completed (from the original) with the date, and details of the parties' execution. Sometimes the drafts were missing in the Dickensian confusion of solicitors' premises. Sometimes those premises had suffered from German bombing, and the relevant papers destroyed. Sometimes the solicitors concerned had moved, changed their firm-name, ignored letters, or were amazingly dilatory about answering. The earlier title could often be established through its being common with adjoining properties, the abstracts of title relating to which could be copied and marked as examined, but enquiries and the work itself were not infrequently laborious. Where a fellow wanted to sell his house, with the title still unreconstituted, the Society might be reviled and its hapless assistant solicitor sorely pressed. But eventually every affected title was duly registered.

Another early chore I look back on with horror was the giving of a series of lectures on mortgage and building society law to those who, like myself, were returning to the 'movement' after years in the Forces. The lectures were under the auspices of the Building Societies Institute, an educational organization, and involved my travelling twice a week for a good few weeks to a lecture room in Moorgate in the City, a tedious journey from our flat in Blackheath, especially in the morning rush-hour. The undertaking is an example of the ardours my absurd conscientiousness has consistently let me in for. I was ill-equipped for the business: for the previous four years I had worked first as a radar mechanic, then as a radar and radio officer, and before that my experience of building society law had extended over little more than two years. I was faced with a class of mainly quite hard-bitten ex-NCOs, all anxious to make up for lost time on coming back into Civvy Street. In later years, visiting local centres of the Building Societies Institute to give a talk (masochism continuing), I might be told by some weighty building society official that he had been in my class at Moorgate, usually saying he had enjoyed the experience, kindly consolation I could have done with at the time. The class was so large, and I suppose my persona so withdrawn, that I was able to identify few individual members. I recall being retrospectively alarmed when I found out that a chap called Robert Hall, a great brain, known in the office as 'the Professor' and who subsequently rose high in the Society's service, had been among my pupils. 'Weren't you ever tempted to contradict me?' I asked him. For I was only a lecture or so ahead of the class, mugging the stuff up just before the deadline. I suppose the advantage for those promising men sent by their societies to refresh their knowledge was that I was able to pass on solutions to problems of comprehension, and that speaking as I did from notes could insert *ad libs* and jokes – a compulsion on any nominally serious occasion, perhaps not always as well received as by those old sweats in Moorgate.

A more agreeable though longer-lasting chore was contributing the 'Legal Notes' to the organ of the building societies movement, the *Building Societies Gazette*, when the previous 'legal correspondent' retired in 1948, though again one is retrospectively surprised at one's Orwell's Boxer-like qualities. Of course, I wrote the monthly 1,500 words or so in the office, where the works of reference were to hand, and was paid a modest but useful fee, and taught myself a lot. The job led to prolonged discussions with the editor and publisher of the *Gazette*, and a building society executive called Herbert Ashworth (later knighted), about a book on mortgages; Herbert to write about the practice side. But at the time he was really too upwardly mobile in his career ever to get down properly to business: with more zip I could have done it all myself, and, looking back, regret not having turned out the book, which in those days would have filled a gap in forensic literature for a volume on mortgage law with a practical slant, and perhaps been less mortal than some of my non-legal output. Later, the enterprise was resumed in collaboration with a fellow solicitor, Gordon Rowe, also in building society service. We got on well but, for reasons that escape me, nothing resulted. It comes to me as I write that I actually completed some chapters of the book – probably nothing great, yet a matter for nostalgia, like all one's consigned-to-the-trunk-in-the-attic works.

As stated, I worked under Fred Shrimpton until 1958. In *The Strange and the Good* I touched on his character – quiet, shrewd, modest, painstaking. I could have wished for no better boss. No doubt, with my liking for things to be cosy, I also suited him. Anyway, we got on marvellously well, never had a cross word – he patient and uncomplaining about my deficiences as a lawyer (for I continued to learn from him long after returning from the Navy), and, what I was probably less conscious of, as a man. The soundness of his professional side was echoed in his private life – a devoted family man; pillar of the Bromley cricket and tennis club; regular at Sundridge Park Golf Club. Some of his habits made a great impression on me. His health and fitness were first-class, but as a younger man he had once suffered an acute attack of quinsy and ever after gargled regularly with glycerine of thymol. For some reason, lost in the mists of tradition, supplies of this rather outmoded specific were obtained for him by the then assistant cashier, Bill Warren.

I think it was not until well after the war that I discovered one of the secrets of Fred's immaculate turn-out. I sometimes wondered at his successful resurrection of what I recognized to be quite venerable suits. It transpired that he subscribed to University Tailors, an organization that regularly collected garments from its clients, cleaned or sponged them (according to need), effected any necessary repairs, and then returned them. Eventually I, too, became a subscriber, maybe not until I had succeeded Fred and felt I could afford the service. I found that even on the lowest scale of subscription one was occasionally hard put to find a suit or overcoat ripe for attention. I was very much reminded of this when after my retirement as the Woolwich solicitor, and I had terminated also my association with University Tailors, I heard from one of the Woolwich executives about Fred's tonsorial habits, hitherto unknown to me. After luncheon in the office, in the room that latterly doubled for Jack Lindsay's office, he invariably went for a walk, I think usually up on to Woolwich Common – probably as far as the parade-ground of the Royal Artillery Barracks, which, with the façade of the buildings behind it, was a spectacle comparable to Leningrad, according to Pevsner. It seems that as frequently as once a week he varied this by a visit, in another direction, to the barbering department of the Royal Arsenal Cooperative Society. There he was always attended to by the senior barber, and he it was who long after Fred's retirement told the executive referred to, the topic having by chance come up, how difficult it was every week to find enough material for his scissors and clippers to work on over a time justifying the fee charged, though Fred retained a quite decent amount of hair into old age.

He lived on until his ninetieth year. I saw him occasionally, and he remained extraordinarily unchanged. But even he had to yield to time, and at his funeral one of his sons told me I would not have recognized him at the end, a second-hand picture that nevertheless perturbed. When I wrote of him in previous memoirs, I submitted the relevant extracts to his widow, Muriel, in case I had got anything wrong. In return she sent a note Fred had written 'in perfect shorthand' (though some of the words were smudged) in 1916, which she had found with his calling-up papers and photographs of army friends, after his death. Over long years of collaboration and friendship with Fred it had emerged that in the First World War he had been a machine-gunner, later a dispatch-rider (and he once related a bizarre military action in the former capacity in some chalk tunnels in France) but he was not given to reminiscing about his experiences. The note that follows was written by little more than a boy; indubitably father to the man.

On Friday 30 June I went into trenches with [illegible] for a very hot time in Hepaterne. [illegible] went down with shell shock. We stayed in our lines until 7.30 next morning, Sat. 1 July, when we went over the top to the Hun's line at Gommecourt and took three lines fairly easily although they made a big stand – held them until dinner time. They then bombed us out to the first Hun line where we were until 7.30 pm when we had to retire across the open to our own lines. The brigade caught up and we lost about 32 men including most of my pals.

I left the Hun line about 9.15 pm and ran to the Headquarters where they gave me room and afterwards in H. I slept until morning. On Sunday morning 8 of us left.

I stayed with the quarter-master for that night.

As Muriel said in the accompanying letter, 'when Fred wrote an article it took him a long time – he was not a born writer'. This *aide mémoire* was almost certainly made and kept because it recorded the killing of his friends: it was shorthand in another sense.

The work coming my way as assistant solicitor was surprisingly varied, not excluding some advocacy, a field Fred detested and left to me. Just after the war, when investors' money rolled in, the Society had made a number of large mortgage advances on the security of commercial property. This business in the main had come *via* a member of the Board called G. Leslie Wates, a West End solicitor whose firm had connections with the world of leisure and entertainment. Some of these mortgage advances eventually fell into arrears, and when the Society had to exercise its power of sale or receivership the position was far from straightforward. What, say, had seemed at the time of the advance a flourishing hotel, the growing habit of holidaying abroad had changed into a white elephant. Trying to spare the Society losses in such cases, I worked closely with the second-in-command of what was then known as advance department, another mighty brain called George Swainsbury. Later, I went on to collaborate with him over the radical revision of the Society's printed mortgage and other forms. I thought of myself as quite a good legal draftsman, but undoubtedly the bulk of the ideas and some of the care came from George. I loved his visits to my room, the discussion sometimes prolonged into philosophical realms. He was an independent thinker, of a rigour (the comparison is not exaggerated) that reminded me of Enoch Powell's, in a time of practically universal leftism.

When in the mid-Fifties I wrote a novel about a building society, *Image of a Society*, I used for part of the plot the failure of a commercial security. I had to invent run-down premises in Paddington, rather an improbable security in the first place, to avoid writing about what had gone wrong in reality with the Woolwich mortgages. Similarly, I had to transform the physical appearance of the demon Vice-Chairman in the novel so that he should not be identified with Leslie Wates.

The latter, well turned-out in a conservative way, authoritative, grey-haired, prosperous, was an unlikely solicitor to have clients owning hotels, bars, 'amusements'. Ancestors of his with

the same surname had been founding fathers of the Society back
in the mid-nineteenth century. He himself had been a prizeman
(an outstanding honour) at one of the Law Society's qualifying
examinations, and carried this academic side of the law into his
role as a director of the Society. There is no doubt that in one
(perhaps large) sense he was a fine lawyer, but in the end I came
to think his judgement in this area less good than he thought it
was. (His putting up commercial securities of the kind that
caused trouble must also be held against him.) Once, in Fred's
absence on holiday, Sandy posed a question to me in writing,
the answer to which had to go before the Board. My opinion was
judged by Wates to be unsound. I came across the exchange of
internal memoranda years later, and was compelled to admit to
myself that from a strict legal point of view Wates was right. But
at the time I (naturally) thought he was wrong, and his lawyer's
ability rankled. Besides, the question was one of those, familiar
to all in-house lawyers, which are better decided in favour of
what their client wants reasonably to do. In a much later matter,
when I had succeeded Fred, I remember reading a long and
well-written opinion of Wates's which I was convinced should
not be followed (nor was it, in some way without giving him
offence). Though he was feared, as in the case of Sandy I got on
quite well with him, on one occasion, with Kate, being invited
out to his house near Wilmington, where he lived in some style.
I suppose discovering his wife to have artistic interests did me
no harm. Nevertheless, Leslie Wates was another whose
absence made life seem easier.

3

When I think back to that decade following the war, a sense of
arduousness and discomfort comes to me, though since I was
comparatively young I must be interpolating to some extent the
standards and style of later life. Still, many must regard with
awe what they had to undergo when making their way in the
world. It would be out of place to write fully about my health,
yet something more must be said. Even as a very young man my
digestion left much to be desired. I discovered as an articled

clerk that beer did not suit me, a social disadvantage at that time. Apart from the two months of the introductory training course, when I was fitter than I had ever been (or have been since), my time in the Navy was attended by indigestion and insomnia, for neither of which conditions did it occur to me to 'report sick', though I am sure that at times an X-ray would have revealed a duodenal ulcer. Amazing, that if I had played my cards right I might have been discharged during the war, possibly with a pension. I should add that mostly I have *looked* well: as I came in due course to jest: 'I *am* well, apart from my ailments.'

After the war, as already recounted, an ulcer was duly revealed by 1948, the year of my other's death, petty concern of health when she was in the last stages of carcinoma. The bland diet prescribed had little effect in the long run on my condition. In 1951 or '52 I was flattered to be asked by the PEN to edit, with Clifford Dyment and Montagu Slater, the first of a series of annual volumes of new poetry. It must have been one of the earliest general recognitions (modest enough) of my presence on the literary scene. The Secretary of PEN was Hermon Ould. When the editors conferred at the PEN premises in Chelsea, Hermon offered sherry, but abstained himself. It soon emerged he was being treated for a duodenal ulcer, but his diet, far from bland, included steaks, salads, and, indeed, battered plaice on the bone, fried and eaten cold, in the Jewish way, familiar to me from boyhood days. This revolutionary regime had been prescribed by a Dr J.-J. Spira, whom Hermon had been put on to by reading a book called *How I Cured My Duodenal Ulcer*, written, under a *nom de plume*, by none other than the prospective publisher of the PEN anthology, Michael Joseph.

The book was tremendously persuasive, not only as an account of a man in chronic discomfort subsisting on an anaemic diet, who was transformed utterly, but also in its portrait of Dr Spira, a Frenchman by origin, described as owning a pianist's sensitive hands, and a highly reassuring and authoritative clinical manner. The secret of the regime prescribed was its low fat content, the theory being that peptic ulcers were caused through the mingling of bile and gastric acid

59

(to put the thing at its simplest). Much later I read Dr Spira's large technical volume on the subject, published by the medical division of Butterworth & Co. He once told me with pride the huge number of references it contained, perhaps the most convincing a study of the incidence of peptic ulcer among labourers recruited for some project in the Far East – one race, I think Chinese, with a high fat diet; the other, probably the indigenous population, with a low fat diet, and coming out much the better.

Poor Hermon failed to benefit from the diet, for his digestive trouble turned out to be a fatal stomach cancer, not diagnosed until too late. But I had been sold on the system by Michael Joseph's book, and consulted Dr Spira. One visited him in his ground-floor flat in a modern block at the Park Lane end of Curzon Street – expensive premises, but on one occasion he said to me with amusement that he had contradicted a fellow West End medico, who was himself advancing the claim, with the words: '*I* am the most expensive doctor in London.' I am sure Spira in my case tempered his fees to the shorn lamb (I think he liked the idea of treating a poet) – it was long before enlightened employers provided their staff with private medical insurance. At any rate, I went on consulting him over a good few years, though I tergiversated about his theory (in fact, while sticking rigidly to the regime in early days I manufactured a gastric as well as – or in lieu of – a duodenal ulcer, extremely painful: he was dumbfounded). But he possessed excellent qualities as a general physician: when I had an inguinal hernia he insisted on my consulting the eminent Dickson Wright, a surgeon (he said) who would ensure what was not always the case, that the repair never came apart. As I was wheeled into the operating theatre, I saw Spira hovering above me, to my surprise, gowned ready to accompany me: he had taken the trouble to find out the time of the operation, and journey from Curzon Street to St Mary's Hospital.

The initial part of Spira's therapy was to give a new patient phenobarbitone to quiet his nerves, the highly-strung being particularly prone to peptic ulceration. On one visit, quite late in my own treatment, he gave me a couple of phenobarbitone tablets after initially taking my pulse, waiting to take it again when they had had effect. The existence of my 'nerves' was proved – I must try to learn to relax – but as a matter of fact I was already suffering (undoubtedly had suffered for years) from thyrotoxicosis (or Graves's Disease), inherited from my mother, though it was not diagnosed until some years further on, when a hand tremor had developed, with intermittent fibrillation. The surgeon at the local hospital, to whom I was referred by my GP, wanted to perform a partial thyroidectomy, but I felt I could not let things proceed without reference to Spira, a characteristic instance of my 'loyalty' (or perhaps undue deference to authority). At first he doubted the diagnosis, and sent me to St Thomas' Hospital for my blood to be checked again. When the gland's mischief was confirmed, I am sure I was influenced by Spira's prejudice against surgery (almost certainly arising from his conviction of its inutility in the treatment of peptic ulcer) by choosing drugs to neutralize the hyperactivity (which I take to this day) rather than the thyroidectomy which my mother underwent in the primitive times of the operation, or a therapeutic dose of radioactive iodine. This was a wrong decision, since in due course there developed a constant (atrial) fibrillation, an additional health nuisance.

To check the date, I have got down from the shelf that first PEN anthology, *New Poems 1952*. To the contemporary poetry buff it is an interesting collection, though I say it myself. Submissions were invited by PEN without restriction, that being an epoch before it was realized how many unpublished poets and poems existed in these islands. I remember going into the front room in Glebe Place and seeing a rather broken-down settee rendered even more broken-down by the weight of the MSS that had come in – epics and book-length collections as well as more modest submissions. Nevertheless, almost all fell to be rejected, and we were forced to write to well-known names to make a publishable anthology. One of the sparse accepted submissions was from Kingsley Amis: in the notes on contributors he described himself as 'working on a novel set in a provincial university'. Another new contributor was Raymond

Richardson: I remember coming across his poems with relief and pleasure at finding something from the settee worthy of printing. They were his first published work, but I think he was sadly not heard of again. Two poets whose contributions I feel sure I solicited were N. K. Cruickshank, whose impressive first (and I rather think only) book of original verse, *In the Tower's Shadow*, I had reviewed on the BBC's Third Programme a few years before; and George Lamming, whose poems I had admired when he had sent them soon after the war to the BBC's *Caribbean Voices*, for which I did some work for a time. Elder poets included Walter de la Mare and Edwin Muir; younger, John Montague and W. S. Merwin. The editors got on well together. Monty Slater, librettist of *Peter Grimes* (would that Britten had stuck to him!), I knew already: like mine, his taste had been mainly formed by the left-wing poets of the Thirties. In that era I had envied Clifford Dyment for being included at a precocious age in the *Faber Book of Modern Verse*. When I met him at the PEN he was utterly unlike my conception of him, being plump, balding, modest, 'nice'. Poor (one says again) Clifford: he lost his beloved wife Marcella, and died himself, at too early an age.

The other great source, in the post-war decade, of what seems now anxiety and inconvenience, was the flat I had taken while I was still a naval officer at the Admiralty at the fag-end of the war. It had many advantages – roominess, easy access to a spacious garden, a controlled rent that more and more, as the years passed, seemed to be a bargain. The flat above had been requisitioned by the local Council during the war, and at first was occupied by a respectable couple and their grown-up daughter. They sometimes sounded to be dropping a few pairs of heavy boots late and early, but otherwise were ideal neighbours. The occupants of the basement flat below were successively ideal – indeed, with the last of these, 'Butch' Baker and his wife, Bunny, we formed a lasting friendship. Butch came out of the RAF with the rank of Group-Captain, then had a second distinguished career as a civil servant, remarkable fate for a bomber pilot.

Through the entropic principle, applicable to many areas of

human life, the flat above fell into the hands first, of representatives of the *lumpen-proletariat* who made noise and floods; then, of the cocky and quarrelsome side of the working class, who hung washing out in the garden but declined to help work at its upkeep. How the basement flat came to be occupied by foreign students, some of the Muslim persuasion, who during Ramadhan kept us awake even longer than the Christians above, would be too tedious to recount. In short, as we moved into middle-age we longed for a detached house, centrally heated (for the great, frigid spaces of our flat were warmed by no more than a coal fire and a few electric bars). We looked at many properties in Blackheath, found them all too large, decayed or conventional; and at last, in 1954, bought part of the garden of a Victorian house in the very road where our flat was, and caused a modest bungalow to be built on it. The plot fronted on what was little more than an unmade rural lane, and though over the years it has been developed and taken on more of the characteristics of suburbia, it has served to funnel some nature into my verse, lifeblood verse seems to require.

Finally, looking back, I marvel somewhat at facing the plod of being second-in-command – inevitably dogsbodyish – of what was quite a large solicitor's office. Though a lawyer like the Kafkaesque Philip Witt in *Image of a Society* must not be envisaged, my heart was not in many of the matters that came my way. Instructions for a lease or purchase of premises for the Society often resulted in a series of moves as boring as those of an early-drawn chess game. If I had thought I could have earned a living eking out my modest royalties with such chores as editing the PEN anthology, I suppose I should have gone over to the literary life. I say 'modest' and so they were, yet my first few novels, though never really 'catching on', came out also in the United States, and earned a bit in subsidiary rights. But had I ever the confidence that I should be able regularly to turn out prose fiction? For me, prose seemed to be almost as much at the mercy of the Muse as poetry.

4

The early Fifties was the time when I started to visit West End galleries, rather more flush with money than hitherto; wanting a few works of art on the great walls of our Victorian ground-floor flat. I soon discovered Helen Lessore's Beaux Arts gallery in Brunton Place. You entered it *via* a lobby, where a few works were hung, then climbed an awkward staircase to a barn-like room which housed the main exhibits, always of interest. The gallery was starting to show what became known as the 'kitchen-sink school' – Jack Smith, John Bratby, Derrick Greaves, Edward Middleditch – and also a number of other painters whose representational style appealed to me. I suppose draughtsmanship was the quality I admired most, greatly to the fore in the Middleditch exhibitions. From that of 1954, the choice encouraged by Helen Lessore's advice, I bought a large oil-on-board, 'Sleep'. It was an epoch when the artist was evidently far from flush, for having got my name and address from the Beaux Arts, he asked me to his studio where I bought, cheaply even for those days, two charcoal drawings displaying the draughtsmanship I loved. A couple of years later I bought another charcoal drawing from his second Beaux Arts show, but his style was starting to change in a way that seemed to me somewhat dubious, and I acquired nothing more of his.

Twenty years after that studio encounter, over the drinks preceding a Royal Academy banquet, a man, seemingly in late middle-age, came up and addressed me by my Christian name. I did not know him from Adam. It was Edward Middleditch, whose painter's eye had recognized me through the accretions of time. We exchanged friendly words until separated by social duties. And a further ten years on I was asked by the Arts Council to lend my Middleditches for a travelling retrospective, which I did. Alas, Ed died only days after the tour had begun. It turned out that ill-health had dogged him for years and seriously affected his working powers. When the exhibition reached the Serpentine Gallery in the spring of 1988, I went to the private view, there once more encountering Helen Lessore (after what seemed a lifetime), who had written an illuminating essay for the catalogue. Both catalogue and exhibition were of great beauty, and I could have kicked myself for not acquiring any of the later work, which now seemed a logical and remarkable extension of the earlier.

1954 and 1956 were also the years of two exhibitions at the Beaux Arts by Raymond Mason, a sculptor who was an outstanding draughtsman as well. Even at that time his sculptures (mainly bas-reliefs as I recall) were beyond my pocket, but I bought a pen and wash study for a terra-cotta – strange figures lined up before a mysterious doorway, just my cup of tea. That must have led to Helen Lessore introducing me to the artist, then in his very early thirties – friendly, talkative in the remains of a Midlands accent, a French girl (herself an artist) in tow. Though I was initially cagy, not at all convinced that I wanted to take our relations further, as was apparently in his mind, it turned out that I asked him to the Victorian flat aforesaid to draw my portrait (and a couple of years later, that of my son). I think I must have got to know that in earlier days he had supported himself for a time by drawing likenesses. The sitting, the first ever undertaken, impressed me, and resulted in a pair of sonnets, 'Sitting for a Portrait', that started:

> Committed to your impersonal scrutiny,
> The searching eyes that look at mine unseeing,
> I fear your verdict on my anatomy:
> 'There is a growth upon your inmost being.'

As for the portrait, after an hour or so's work, Raymond went to the bathroom and to our dismay washed it, or what he could of it, off. He said he would do another in his studio – which was in Paris, for with his asthma he found it impossible to live in England. True to his word, a masterly sepia and black wash-drawing eventually turned up: with a stroke of insight he had depicted the subject looking out through a window, his hand against the pane.

Many years later Raymond gave us the refurbished original drawing, and that is the one used for the jacket of *New and Collected Poems 1934–84*. By that time, despite geographical separation, he had become a firm friend, never neglecting to see or call us when in England. His views on the duty of art to reality and humanity coincided with mine. For far too long his work was neglected over here, though his reputation in France and the United States was high. Amends started to be made when the Arts Council in 1983 put on a wonderful retrospective at the Serpentine Gallery and the Oxford Museum of Modern Art.

Apropos of my reunion with Edward Middleditch, transferred by time into a Royal Academician, one ought to emphasize the Proustian powers of the annual Royal Academy banquets, two of which I attended in the Seventies. One says Proustian, but Powellian is the more appropriate epithet, for in *Hearing Secret Harmonies* Tony acutely anatomized the function – 'a kind of carnival, devoted to the theme of Past and Present' – and used it for one of the most amazing strokes in *A Dance to the Music of Time*, the identification of the anonymous figure at Sillery's Oxford tea-party of donkey's years before. In real life, as he once told me, he had had a scarcely less astonishing experience – a discussion about Apollinaire with Mrs Thatcher.

At my first banquet I found myself seated at dinner opposite Constance Cummings. Though she was a year or two older than me she had by no means lost the looks that had attracted me long before the war. I was a fan, and through my knowledge was able to demonstrate it, so we got on well. At my second banquet I had a similar encounter with another, much younger American actress who had become anglicized, the beauteous Gayle Hunnicutt. I set the ball rolling by speaking of something quite *recherché* and ingratiating – her stunning appearance a good few years before in a TV adaptation of Henry James's *The Ambassadors* – and our converse endured as we left the table at the end of dinner. Time was getting on, and I had planned not to miss the last 53 bus home, then a dicier service than later. Though it seemed churlish to abandon my *vis-à-vis*, I saw a providential opportunity when we encountered the solid bearded figure of the *cinéaste* Colin Young, whom I had got to know through his membership of the BBC's General Advisory Council. I introduced them, and left Burlington House with an easy conscience – thoroughly Fullerian parting.

5

Succeeding Fred as the Society's solicitor in 1958 proved not to be quite the automatic process anticipated. The Board was familiar with, or had been specifically told of, my dubious health, required reassurance that I should be able to stand up to the responsibilities of the new appointment. Sandy wrote me a memorandum asking me to make an appointment to see Sir Adolphe Abrahams – 'a quite elderly physician' in Sandy's phrase, words that stick in my mind, but (he went on to say in words I have forgotten) one whose judgement he and the Board would unhesitatingly accept. Sir Adolphe, brother of Harold, the great athlete, was in fact a supreme example of the elements in Sandy's life, like Pilgrim House and matches and wooden pencils, in which he had implicit faith. Somewhere along the line, Sir Adolphe had been recommended to him, whereupon Sandy had appropriated the eminent doctor to himself.

I went to see Sir Adolphe in Harley Street; the ambience dingy, worn-out, re-encountered in subsequent visits to other consultants, quite unlike Spira's Curzon Street premises. But Sir Adolphe himself was spry, agreeable and civilized, and very soon we passed from the physical to matters of culture, he perhaps having been furnished by Sandy with details of my literary *alter ego*. A few days after, Sandy wrote again to me, saying that Sir Adolphe's report was wholly satisfactory, and confirming my appointment.

I was immensely fortunate in inheriting, with Fred's job, a staff of experienced managing and other clerks, many of whom had been with the solicitor's department since leaving school. A wonderful *esprit de corps* existed, nurtured by Fred's stressless style of leadership, and a tradition of parties and amateur theatricals on any suitable occasion (Leslie Vosper, one of the managing clerks, was a talented conjuror, member of the Magic Circle). How much the staff of the department became a part of one's life! Umpteen years on, I could delineate in detail the physiognomies and characters of most of its members in my time, Shakespearean in their variety and Englishness. As in any collection of sixty or seventy individuals, there were a couple of awkward customers, with whom Fred and his senior managing clerk ('office manager', as the title became) had undoubtedly been too lenient over the years. Each in his own way was irascible and pig-headed, getting on the wick of outside solicitors with whom they came in contact, unheeding of rebuke. Yet when I myself had to try to neutralize these thorns in the flesh, I found in them quite touching virtues, well-concealed generosity and kindness, though I did not lament the day when at last they came up to retirement.

Fred had trained the younger of one of the pairs of brothers, Harold Kemble, to be his personal assistant. Before the war, Fred had acted for an astutely speculative member of his wife's family who had bought a large landed estate or two, on the market because of the incidence of death duties, and sold them off in a number of separate lots before the purchase price for the whole estate was due to be paid. Harold had cut his teeth on this complex and urgent work, and become a meticulous conveyancer for whom no transaction was too 'heavy'. Moreover, he was knowledgeable in most practical affairs of life, among other things an outstanding gardener and handyman. After we had both retired I was troubled with a squeaking refrigerator door, unamenable to oil. I was due to attend the annual dinner for old Woolwich employees; said to Kate I would there ask Harold's advice, which I did. He at once prescribed a drop of washing-up liquid on the hinge. Needless to say, it did the trick. On succeeding Fred, I kept Harold as right-hand man, plugging my deficiencies.

As assistant solicitor I had been sustained by a young man called John Dyer. Not very long after the war my secretary told me that a boy was returning to the office who had been called up for National Service while I myself was in the Navy, so unknown to me. Though he had never been much more than an office boy, Mrs Rider said he was promising material, and that I ought to take him on as my personal assistant. What an eye for a winner! John proved to be utterly reliable, anxious to learn his trade, and developed into another sound conveyancer. Years later, when we were on more equal terms, he told me of his anxieties and struggles with the tasks I piled on him, often out of the usual run of the department's work. He had read my autobiographies, and compared his position *vis-à-vis* me with my position as a young solicitor with Harold E. Pain, as described in *The Strange and the Good*. Also it was only in later years that I discovered he was a keen book collector, Dornford Yates a good example of his rather Usbornesque taste. He was one who married a fellow member of the department, and lived happily ever after.

Fred had been Chairman of the Building Societies Association's legal advisory panel, a more or less honorary job that also passed to me. The Association was the movement's professional organization, and the panel's chairmanship made me in effect its legal adviser. Of course, during Fred's time I had seen the scope of the work, and often helped him with it, for we worked in close collaboration, in adjoining rooms. Building societies grew in size, as eventually did the legislation affecting them: the work for the Association took up more and more of my time. Just before Fred retired we recruited a solicitor of twenty-eight (who luckily for the Society had not found the niche his talents deserved) to take my place as assistant solicitor. Mark Preston was an ideal complement to me: careful and thorough where I was quick and slapdash, able to take on work that would have fallen to me had it not been for Association affairs. Also, he could sing Tom Lehrer and other comic songs at the piano, a great asset in the department's beanos.

When I took over the Legal Advisory Panel, the BSA's Secretary-General was a former Territorial and wartime Colonel called Charles Garrett-Holden. At once, to get to know me better, he asked me to lunch at his club, which was the Cavalry and Guards Club in Piccadilly, commonly known as the 'In and Out' on account of the two words, one at each end of the semi-circular drive-way in front of the entrance door. Readers of my earlier memoirs may recall my experience of another West End services club. Nevertheless, despite this initiation, the occasion with G-H (as he was universally referred to), modest though it might be thought, was a memorable part of my elevation to an order of conduct and responsibility substantially different from that appropriate to the Society's assistant solicitor. (Many years later I renewed my acquaintance with the In and Out, when I was taken there for lunch a few times by John Lehmann in his more parsimonious days. He had resigned from the Garrick Club, which he said was too expensive. I asked him how he came to belong to the In and Out, an unlikely choice for one whose war service was confined to fire-watching. He said his father, R. C. Lehmann, of *Punch* and the River, had put him up; strange link with the Edwardian past.) Another luncheon venue I came to be taken to was a kind of private restaurant in Park Lane, used by the Association (whose offices were then in Park Street) for more or less working lunches with members of its Council – a body composed mainly of the chief executives of the leading building societies. But by that time any sense of awe at the company or location had virtually disappeared.

Fred Shrimpton had had quite an easy time as Chairman of the Legal Advisory Panel. There had been no specifically building society legislation since 1940. Everything changed soon after I took over. Financial unsoundness in the building society world compelled the Government to bring in a statute (The Building Societies Act 1960) to control the very type of mortgage lending that my own Society had dabbled its toes in after the war – and to tighten controls in other directions. The Association had to watch the legislation at all stages, and try to secure what it conceived to be necessary practical amendments. It was my first experience of encountering senior civil servants and Members of Parliament, and of legislative procedures. Two years later, building society legislation was consolidated in the Building Societies Act 1962: again, much work came my way.

The man in charge of legal matters at the Association was G. L. B. Pitt, a barrister who I think had never practised; also with a chartered secretary qualification. I could not have asked for a more agreeable *vis-à-vis*, and over the years I grew very fond of him. Like Mark Preston, he was a foil – infinitely painstaking, phenomenally thorough. We had a past in 'the Andrew' in common, though he had seen active service as a supply officer in big ships, whereas I had skulked in shore establishments in the Fleet Air Arm. He had retained his interest in Navy vessels, become quite an expert, had at least one letter in *The Times* about the Fleet's strength and composition. Bespectacled, with rather Punch-like features, serious, but always ready for jokes and exchange of gossip, he nobly did his duty by the Association, turning out vast circulars of guidance to its member societies (many of them small and lacking specialized legal advice), testing the traditional rigidities of the civil servants in the Registry of Friendly Societies and the relevant Ministries. When matters of difficulty arose, he would come on the telephone to me at Woolwich for marathon conversations: it is a tribute to his character that I endured – even enjoyed – them.

Graham Pitt, when I first knew him, was a devoted cigarette smoker, as was I. Suddenly, he gave the habit up, weaning himself on Fox's Glacier Mints, the unwrapping of one of which would be the preliminary to some knotty problem. I used to think I might one day write, not about Graham's character and appearance, but the complexities of legislation and parliamentary procedure, and the public and semi-public figures encountered. When I retired as the Society's solicitor I did indeed bring home a few files, from which the subtleties of the work might have been recovered. But as the years have passed, not only has memory dimmed, but also the depiction of that sort of reality has for me lost much of its value and interest, though I see it could be vivified by being cast in fictional form. (Some recent published diaries of politicians – Crossman, for example, and Tony Benn – have in fact portrayed well the amazingly detailed texture of the life of affairs.) As to the great of that world, only a few detached memories float to the surface. I recall being introduced by Graham to the first Lord Milner of Leeds in the lobby of the House of Lords. He was a Labour peer, a solicitor, due to speak on behalf of the Association in a debate on the Building Societies Bill of 1960, probably a Vice-President of the Association. We discussed briefly some provision the Association considered unfair to, or unworkable by, building societies. Then we all went into the chamber, and quite soon I was surprised to hear, from the spectators' pen, much of what I had said flow more or less verbatim from Lord

Milner's lips. Another memory, vivid but imprecise, is of Crossman, living up to his name at a meeting at the Ministry of Housing and Local Government (of which he was then the head), and being brought a note which caused him to leave at once without a word. It was the moment of his being summoned to 10 Downing Street to take a higher Government post, he being actually in expectation of the sack (I feel sure the episode is related in his diaries).

It must have been towards the end of 1964 that I was invited by the Law Society to become a member of a 'Working Party on Conveyancing', to be set up by the Society to make proposals for the simplification and speeding-up of conveyancing of real property. I felt very flattered; had to get Sandy Meikle's consent (and he may well have put it to the Board) to my devoting some of the Woolwich's time to the project. He rather regarded the thing as an honour for the Woolwich, which it was, for it had really been the pioneer among building societies in setting up an in-house legal department. The Law Society was the disciplinary body for solicitors, as well as their professional organization; so few solicitors regarded it otherwise than with awe or antagonism.

The invitation had come in a letter from the Law Society's Secretary-General, Sir Thomas Lund, whom I had actually met socially once or twice, without really knowing him. The Working Party meetings took place in the Law Society's Hall in Chancery Lane, at first fortnightly in the afternoons; then, as the magnitude of the task became evident, starting in the mornings. There were no more than a dozen of us: bonhomie and leg-pulling rapidly developed. Though among us was a solicitor-lecturer from the Law Society's School of Law, and several members of the Society's staff, most of the Party were working solicitors, some from famous practices. It had been donkey's years – since before the war – that I had come into such close contact with members of my profession, sealed off both by war service and becoming an in-house lawyer, with merely one client. The renewed intercourse was stimulating and reassuring. Common training and experience promoted an ease and shorthand of communication: it may sound pi, but one was convinced afresh of the essential honourableness, even self-abnegation of the profession, to say nothing of the brain-power of its best members. I recall being astounded by a masterly paper prepared by Ridley Peecock (a busy Slough solicitor), for a sub-committee of the Party, formulating the awful problems (with solutions) of the enforcement of negative and positive covenants affecting land.

Many of us still smoked cigarettes in those unenlightened days, none more religiously than Tommy Lund, a Player's Medium Navy Cut man. He also usually appeared, lunch-time and evening, in the bar of the Law Society's Hall, to listen to members' gossip and grouches, and to retail his own news and anecdotes. The barmaids had instructions that after I think five gins they were to serve him silently with tonic-water alone. He was also greatly in demand as an after-dinner speaker, an art at which he excelled, unlike many with a reputation in that tricky field. I wondered how he stood up to this gruelling regime, until after a little while on the Working Party I learnt from him that on his way to the office every morning he stopped off at the Marylebone Public Baths, and did a specific number of lengths, battling his way through schoolchildren.

The vision evoked was more than faintly ludicrous. Tommy was tall, quite heavily built, not much hair, then coming up to sixty. At first glance he was ugly: a curious cast in one eye made his regard somewhat oblique. But his slightly lisping voice was attractive; his speech fluent. Numberless stories – true, apocryphal, smoking-room – had passed, were continually passing, into his retentive brain; and his own invention and observation were fertile. Accordingly, his conversation was phenomenally engaging. From him, in one of the Chancery Lane washrooms, I first heard of the judge's spoonerism that a will must be interpreted through the testicles of the spectator. (No doubt I was an ideal listener to such things, having been so long away from gatherings of lawyers.) Tommy's daughter, also a solicitor, was a friend and adviser of Paul Getty. Tommy, though not playing down the millionaire's idiosyncrasies, provided anecdotal evidence that put him in a favourable light. My few previous encounters with Tommy as fellow public-dinner guests had not prepared me for his authority and resource as a chairman of committee. Nor was he really outclassed by the learning and experience of those he chaired, though his practical conveyancing lay far in the past, for he had joined the staff of the Law Society in 1930, the year after his admission as a solicitor. In short, he was one of those rare men one is reassured to find in both public and private spheres, a contrast to most politicians.

Through membership of the Working Party, and the work for the BSA, I began, against all the odds, and most of my previous experience, to enjoy the practice of the law. I had sometimes been 'stretched' before – in complicated conveyancing or litigation, teasing draftsmanship, understanding and advising the Society on knotty problems (following Fred's tradition, I rarely consulted counsel) – but in this outside work I was stretched in an agreeable way. In the case of the BSA there was a sense that one's labours were essential to the workings of what had become a large segment of the financial world – and a segment conducted not for profit, and that involved millions of householders and small investors. One began to get to know, too, the not entirely uncomic, not unimpressive (Shakespearean, Dickensian!) workings of British governance – for instance, making one's way through a courtyard beyond the entrance to the Lords to the offices of the Lord Chancellor's Department, there, with Graham, to keep an appointment with the second senior civil servant, Mr Boggis-Rolfe. Graham, in his correspondence, would omit the title (it was before the feeble days of Christian names) – 'Dear Boggis-Rolfe' and (more strikingly, in a way, through some vague but aristocratic Germanic association) 'Dear Volmar', Volmar being senior legal man at the Registry of Friendly Societies, whom Graham had known over a good few years. It emerged that his Christian name was Adelbert, but I doubt if Graham ever addressed him as such, in writing or otherwise.

I came to admire, in a way, that sacerdotal caste, senior civil servants – rather as in my boyhood I admired Makepeace, the noted Lancashire stone-waller. To say no, and to go on saying no, under the pressure of excellent arguments from able men

74

requires great will-power and complete absorption of tradition. Combined with this there must be an ability to keep the nose scrupulously clean, and a conventionality so complete that at moments it may seem revolutionary. When I joined the Society's Board in 1969 I became the colleague of two such former priests, Sir George Ismay and Sir Edmund Compton. George, and his elegant wife Jeanne, we liked and got to know quite well. He had been recruited to the Board by the Chairman, Sir Thomas Spencer, who was also Chairman of Standard Telephones (to which post he had risen from the ranks). Tommy had come across him through George's final office as Deputy Director-General of the Post Office. The parochial nature of English life was well illustrated when I discovered that George Rostrevor Hamilton had been George Ismay's boss when, both of them then at the Treasury, they served the Twenties Colwyn Committee on taxation in a secretarial capacity.

As a matter of fact, George Ismay was far less of an establishment figure than Edmund Compton: he was a Cumbrian or north Lancastrian, who had served in the ranks during the First World War, winning the Military Medal. He had a good brain; kept his own statistics about the Society's financial progress. He passed these papers on to me when he retired, but I lacked the drive and capacity to keep the figures up to date. During our mutual time on the Board we sat next to each other, myself on the seat farther from the head, being the newer member. We agreed in many matters of threatened or actual folly or unsoundness, though in one course of action he had become notorious rather than famous. He had persuaded the Society to invest in a longer-dated Government stock than was normal, his argument being that such a high return was unlikely to be seen again. Alas, this was merely the start of an epoch of high interest rates, and the Society had to wait until the stock approached its redemption date before seeing it rise to the price paid. Round the Board table the stock became jocularly and generically known as 'the Ismays' ('the Daltons' as precedent).

Apropos of Sir Thomas Spencer, I have used the cognomen 'Tommy', but I never called him that to his face. He had been on the Board since 1944, so I had known him in my assistant solicitor days. Later on, probably after I had passed Sir Adolphe Abrahams's inspection, he quite often alluded to my improved appearance, affecting to have once seen me a thin, unhealthy specimen of humanity. My apparent recovery in his eyes from that state did not at all lessen my displeasure when such remarks were made, and I was conscious at once of their substratum of truth, and that I still fell short of his physical ideal. Besides, I suspected that the observation was to some extent prompted by a cock-up I had made when conducting the conveyancing of Tommy's house-purchase not long after my return from the war. I had been outsmarted by the solicitor acting for the vendor, and Fred Shrimpton nobly went to see Tommy to explain, and apologize for, the mess. For me it was heavily embarrassing (one of those perhaps three or four ghastly events which I suppose occur in every life), and continued to be so for some time, despite the fact that eventually the cock-up (a technicality needless to explain) proved to have no deleterious consequences for Tommy or his house.

Tommy himself spoke as one who enjoyed phenomenal good health, and took precautions to preserve it. When I became solicitor and lunched with the Board on Board days, I could not fail to observe that for pudding there was invariably placed before him a plate containing an apple and a knife (the latter called for because his teeth were not his own). I also noticed that he allowed cups of tea and coffee to cool inordinately, and much later on I think this habit came up for discussion, possibly provoked by me, he advancing the plausible theory that hot fluids were carcinogenic. At the time of my conveyancing mishap he would have been barely sixty, but after I had joined the Board and got to know him best, he often spoke of 'passing through the sound barrier', rather as the secret of human well-being. For a time the expression remained enigmatic; then I realized he was referring to passing his eightieth birthday. In his ninth decade his grasp of matters coming before the Board grew to be imperfect, his observations founded on a kind of commonsense; even so, rarely of help. By that time he had relinquished the Chair, and sat as an ordinary member. In appearance he stayed much the same. In his youth he had played on the wing for Woolwich Arsenal, a club that later became 'the' Arsenal, and was said to have been outstanding. He had the bow-legs of many a good soccer player (Charlie Vaughan of Charlton Athletic, and Stanley Matthews come to mind), and retained his erect, slim figure. His moustache was perennially fascinating: clipped short, and so sparse one kept imagining he had shaved it off. At Standard Telephones he eventually became Honorary President, an office created for him, and was driven to the company's premises in the Strand every free day, raising speculation as to what was found for him to do. Still, he was undoubtedly right to cling to office, would have been without resources in retirement.

In the Society's Rules as originally constituted no retirement age for members of the Board was prescribed. It was because a director or two began to look past it (a drooping eyelid here, a rubber-tipped stick there), the unpleasant task of suggesting retirement falling to the current Chairman (or, indeed, lower down the hierarchy), that the Board brought in a standing order that its members should relinquish office at seventy-five. (Later on, legislation laid down a compulsory retirement age of, effectively, seventy.) Accordingly, though my eyelids and gait were normal, I was compelled to go in 1987. I had then served the Society over forty-nine years, and sentimentally would have liked to complete fifty. Otherwise I had few regrets. As a result of the 1986 Building Societies Act, societies were becoming different, and to me, less agreeable animals. Indeed, that statute provides a way for a building society to turn itself into a limited company, with all the consequences of equity share-holders and keeping profits up to the mark. As with so many things in one's lifetime – bread, schooling, dress, manners – the enviable friendly society status, invention by British genius of a fair institution for spreading home ownership, was laid open for destruction. (And just as I write the foregoing, the *Daily Express* of 7 September 1988 reports that the Abbey National Building Society, which was in the process of turning itself into a company, circulated to its members details of a savings/insurance plan, pointing out that one of its benefits was that the life office concerned was a mutual organization, with no shareholders to pay dividends to.)

Of course, I missed some colleagues, and the jokes and beefs round the Board table. The last-named (with its accompanying heavy hide chairs) had been constructed in the Thirties to fit the Boardroom; itself, with its panelling and concealed ceiling lights, a supreme example of then current posh business *décor*. The table was an elongated U. New members started at the end of one or other arm (symmetry in numbers being the aim, though never moving from the arm initially assigned) and, as death (latterly standing orders also) took its toll, moved up towards the curve of the U. I was directed to the arm opposite the windows, and such was the age of the Board when I joined that it seemed no time at all before I had someone on my right – and indeed had moved to a respectable position half way up my arm of the U. But by the time I had reached the bend, and was theoretically in the running if not for Chairman possibly Vice-Chairman, I had too few years to go to put myself among the starters. Not for me the long-term strategy of Sandy's ambition. As a matter of fact, I would not have accepted either office: if I had ever had any aspiration in the business or professional world, by then it was extinguished. Occasionally, as the longest (or longest not holding the current Chairmanship or Vice-Chairmanship) serving director I had temporarily to take the Chair: then it might come over me how things had moved on since I joined the Society as a young man of twenty-six from the provinces, raw edges only slightly cooked by contact with Frank Flower and Mervyn Bompas, notable solicitors encountered in previous employment. It might even occur to me also that with not much flannel I could have passably occupied the high offices spurned.

As to oneself becoming, or looking, gaga, I was lucky enough in my seventies to have stayed the same weight I had been when playing right back for the Blackpool Boys' High School XI, ten stone seven, give a pound or two on occasion. I had also retained my hair. Like my maternal Uncle John I presented in old age a comparatively youthful look. At the last but one Annual General Meeting of the Society I attended I had to second the proposal for the re-election of a fellow member of the Board. Immediately preceding this, a member of the Society had from the body of the hall complained about the advanced age of some of the directors (though the seventy-five years limit was then in force). So when I got up, I said: 'Chairman, ladies and gentlemen, I rise dodderingly to second the proposal . . .' The laugh obtained depended on not being ostensibly doddering.

And as to beefs round the Board table, one was conscious of the irony of having assumed the role of ancient, fuddy-duddy director that in one's executive past one had looked on so pityingly and exasperatedly. Yet long service as non-executive director convinced me of the worth of that office; indeed, that non-executive directors should have the final say. The experience was confirmed by my spell on the BBC Board of Governors.

IV

OXFORD

I

W HEN Edmund Blunden resigned the Oxford Professorship of Poetry in 1968 before his term expired (the
office, though light, had got him down) a number of unsuitable
candidates presented themselves, as previously touched on.
The Chair is a curiosity in that its holder acquires office through
the votes of Masters of Arts of the University, voting in person
in Oxford. No college provides a fellowship, or even rooms, for
the professor, and his main statutory obligation is merely to
lecture three times a year for five years. The stipend is, or was,
commensurate with the burden of the duties: initially in my
time £525 per annum (plus £20 a year from the Creweian
Benefaction, of which more anon).

The candidates might be said to have ranged from Yevtushenko, the Soviet poet, a noted egoist, to a poet of Celtic
origin, who spoke his verse to the playing of a harp by his
daughter, and taking in on the way a young 'pop' poet, not
unknown. One evening my son, a don at Magdalen, was dining
in the company of Maurice Bowra, Warden of Wadham, who
said to him: 'Can't you persuade your father to stand?' I think
almost at the same time a London-based force, in which
Kingsley Amis was prominent, set about nominating me with
an impressive list of supporters. I couldn't but be touched by
this evidence of regard, but now am staggered that I consented
to let my name go forward. I was still in my full-time job as
solicitor to the Woolwich, and, through Sandy, had to obtain
the Board's permission to stand. It would have been easy to
represent to Sandy that though I was sensible of the honour of
the projected nomination, election would adversely affect my

value to the Woolwich: I would then have had a good excuse to put to my supporters. As it was, I made light of the extra duties that would ensue, though I must at least have been slightly daunted by the prospect of delivering fifteen hour-long lectures to a critical audience.

I have somewhere the press cuttings about the run-up to the election, quite numerous. The contest, also plainly not lacking in elements of the ludicrous, appealed to the sporting instincts of the British public. Odds could be obtained about the runners, in the end of almost sufficient number to have permitted each-way betting had they been horses. Some candidates made, or were reported as making, injudicious statements about their beliefs or intentions. I myself did nothing in the way of campaigning, but my son shrewdly ensured that a copy of my *New Poems*, recently published, was deposited in each Oxford Senior Common Room. When the votes were counted I had quite an ample margin over the runner-up, Enid Starkie. Had I known she was going to be a candidate (a perfectly sensible one), and how much she craved a professorship (denied her in her academic career), I may well have declined to stand myself. Not long after the election she dined me at Somerville, plenty of whisky available beforehand; and when I sometimes met her in the Oxford streets (turned out like a diminutive French *matelot*) our exchanges were warm. But the encounters were numbered, for she died in the spring of 1970, after having made light of a long illness.

Indeed, Oxford's welcome was uniformly generous. It surprised me as much as the prestige still attached to the office. My son's old college, New College, matriculated me (and gave me dining rights) so that I could be voted an MA degree by the University; his present college gave me Senior Common Room rights; and the University Registry (ref POE/1) was courteously explicit as to what was required from a tyro Professor of Poetry. One of the first invitations, if not the very first, was to have an evening drink with the Warden of All Souls in his Lodgings. That must have been just after my initial lecture, in which I had referred to the first edition of Matthew Arnold's *Culture and Anarchy* containing a sentence excised from later editions ('As for rioting, the old Roman way of dealing with *that* is always the right one; flog the rank and file, and fling the ring-leaders from the Tarpeian Rock'), for Warden Sparrow reached up to his well-filled shelves, and pulled out *Culture and Anarchy*, and showed me the passage in question. The volume was not only the first edition, but one inscribed by Arnold to, I think, John Ruskin.

I had been directed at the porter's lodge across (or so it seems to me now) the great quadrangle in the fading light, received by the butler at the Lodgings and conducted to the Master's presence in his study. I think only sherry was offered. John Sparrow's was a familiar face, mainly through his appearing in intellectual discussion programmes on TV. The dark, thick hair, parted rather forward from a side parting so that a lock was apt to fall over the brow, had taken on hues of grey. He would then have been in his early sixties. His name had been known to me since the Thirties, when he had earned the opprobrium of Geoffrey Grigson in *New Verse* for pronouncing adversely on modern poetry. Strange, the brief whirligigs of time that had brought us face to face, to say nothing of the whirligigs of taste: I rejoiced in his putting down of those who had ludicrously supported *Lady Chatterley* on moral and artistic grounds in the Penguin trial.

While we talked, the butler brought in a parcel. 'Do you mind if I open this?' Sparrow asked. 'I've been looking forward to its coming.' When the wrapping was removed a substantial album was revealed. It contained large, mounted photographs of undergraduates trying to gain access to All Souls, Sparrow successfully barring their way, no doubt with some auxiliaries. It was the epoch of revolting students: a good reason for the Arnoldian phrase in my lecture striking home. The Warden briefly and gleefully commented on the events depicted at the gates of All Souls. The thwarted invaders had wanted the spacious premises (a post-graduate college) to be opened up to undergraduates; or were possibly there just for the hell of it.

Sparrow himself, on my leaving, conducted me to the aforesaid gates, taking in on our way the splendours of the Codrington Library, in one corner of which sat a solitary

Woolwich executives at Sheffield, 1958. Roy Fuller
third from left, A. E. Shrimpton second from left,
Sir Thomas Spencer second from right.

John Fuller's wedding, 1960. From left to right, Kate
Fuller, Julian Symons, John Fuller.
Photo: Portman Press

Roy Fuller's brother John

Roy Fuller's son John

Jack Clark

John Pudney *Photo: Stanley Graham*

Roy and Kate Fuller (and Domino), Blackheath 1963
Photo: Mark Gerson

Georgina, Valentine and Bonamy Dobrée, outside their Pond Road
house *Photo: Edward Hutton*

Roy and Kate Fuller with Alexander Meikle at the Building Societies
Association Conference, 1970

Roy Fuller, George Howard, Denis Greenhill and Mark Bonham
Carter at the opening of the new BBC Manchester building, 1976

Father and son, Roy and John, at a joint poetry reading, 1985
Photo: Granville Davies

Prizes. C Day Lewis presents the Duff Cooper Memorial Prize,
and, in 1980, Alan Ross presents the Cholmondeley Award
Photo: Gary Ede

Roy Fuller in doctoral robes, Canterbury 1986

scholar. I think I am right in saying that we did not encounter (the cliché is apt) another living soul.

2

One of the duties of the Professor of Poetry enumerated by the Registrar, Sir Folliott Sandford, in his initial letter, was that of delivering the Creweian Oration every other year at the Encaenia (the annual degree-conferring ceremony), to begin in 1970. Perhaps I may quote the entry for 'Creweian Oration' from the edition of *Brewer's Dictionary of Phrase and Fable* of that year:

> A Latin oration delivered in alternate years by the Public Orator and Professor of Poetry at the ENCAENIA of Oxford University, essentially to commemorate the benefactions of Nathaniel, third Baron Crew [*sic*] (1633–1721), Bishop of Oxford and later of Durham. He was a notorious sycophant and a favourite of the Duke of York, afterwards James II. From 1688 he was in disgrace and his benefactions may be regarded as belated attempts to restore his name.

Sir Folliott's paragraph about this obligation in his initial letter (26 November 1968) was a masterpiece of tact:

> I need not at this stage go into details of the procedure which we have adopted for your predecessors in the chair, but you may perhaps like to have a copy of the oration delivered last year by your predecessor in office. I do not think I should be guilty of any indiscretion if I reveal that it is now usual for the Professor to make use of a *domesticum auxilium*. At the end of the Hilary Term in the year in which the Professor is to deliver the oration, I usually write to him (with a copy to his *domesticum auxilium*), to draw attention to any benefactions and honours which I feel he may wish to mention in his oration. The speech is not normally finalized until after the Birthday Honours List. I have had an informal agreement with your predecessors, and also with the Public Orator, that I see the oration in draft. This has enabled me on one or two occasions to suggest the inclusion of items which had been overlooked (and on one occasion to

suggest the deletion of a passage that might have resulted in an action for libel!).

I had decided at an early stage that I would get out of delivering the oration, but had not communicated my intention to the University authorities. At school, though I had dropped Latin in favour of science, I had been old enough to know that what I had been taught was the then still 'new' pronunciation, an example of which, dear to schoolboy hearts, was '*causas*', pronounced 'cow's arse'. When, as a solicitor's articled clerk, I began to study law, I had to get used to the old legal pronunciation of the few Latin phrases commonly in use, such as the writ of *fieri facias*, pronounced by lawyers 'fiery fayshus', 'arse' not involved. Just before the 1969 Encaenia I was able to raise the matter with Sir Folliott:

Stupidly not finding out the date of the Encaenia far enough in advance, I regret I shall not be able to attend this year owing to commitments in London. I have been meaning to write to you, however, about the 1970 Encaenia – and those in 1972 and 1974. My feeling is, after giving the matter much thought, that in my case it is wrong for me to deliver the Creweian Oration. Of course, I realize that nowadays the Professor's role can merely be a parrot-like one, but even this seems quite inappropriate for one whose Latin was left irretrievably behind in a rudimentary state at the age of thirteen. I think I am probably the first holder of the office in this pickle. Recently I came across an unpublished letter of one of my predecessors, A. C. Bradley, to Gilbert Murray, written in July 1901. About the oration he said: 'It was horrible work reading it – the only downright fraudulent thing I have done, I think, since I became a moral being ["about nineteen", Bradley added].' When I think of my knowledge of the tongue, and its quantities and pronunciation, compared with Bradley's, I'm all the more strengthened in my resolve!

I dislike very much breaking with tradition – but the break need not bind my successors. I regret also troubling you and others who may be involved, notably, I suppose, the Public Orator. And I see that I must renounce my share of the Creweian Benefaction – and repay what I have already received from it! On the other hand, I comfort myself with the notion that by not making a mockery of the duty I am leaving it open in the future to be performed with accuracy and grace – and reason.

Sir Folliott's reply a few days later was not only headed POE/1 but also CREWE/1. He expressed regret, and said he would write to me again. We exchanged the following letters later in the summer:

When I acknowledged your letter of 15 June, I said that I should have to do a little research on the arrangements under which the Professor of Poetry has hitherto delivered the Creweian Oration in alternate years.

I find this goes back to an arrangement approved by Convocation on 2 July 1731, when Crewe's domestic chaplain made a deposition of what he knew the Bishop's intentions in making a bequest to the University to have been. One of the provisions was:

'the yearly sum of £40, £20 of which to be paid to the University Orator, the other £20 to the Poetry Lecturer, who in consideration thereof should be obliged alternately to make a speech in commemoration of the benefactors to the University in the Public Theatre once in the year.'

I reported to Council last week the difficulty you foresaw in delivering the Creweian Oration in Latin, and Council agreed that I should ask the Public Orator whether he would be willing to deliver the Oration in 1970 and 1972. This he has agreed to do, and I think it follows that he should, in each of the years during which you are Professor from 1969 onwards, receive the full fee of £40, which has hitherto been divided between the Public Orator and the Professor of Poetry. In your letter of 15th June you offered to repay the £20 which you have already received, but it will be simpler for all concerned if the University Chest deducts it from the next instalment of your emoluments, and I have given the appropriate instructions.

I should perhaps mention that when the matter came before Council last week, there was a suggestion that perhaps the time had come when the Professor of Poetry at least might deliver the Creweian in English rather than in Latin. This would involve legislation, and was clearly not a course to be embarked upon in the middle of the long vacation. I mention it now because it might happen that some time during the next year I might come back to you with a suggestion that you should deliver the Creweian in 1970 and 1972 in English, in which case, of course, the fee arrangements would be revised again and you would receive £40 for each oration you delivered.

I wrote to Sir Folliott in reply:

I'm greatly obliged for your trouble in this affair: the Council's decision is entirely satisfactory and has removed the only misgiving I had about my five years in Oxford. I would be delighted to do the job in English, if later that were to be decided on . . .

I attended the 1970 Encaenia. The formula for those participating in the procession was to gather in a College Hall (this year Brasenose), 'partake of Lord Crewe's Benefaction to the University', and then march in strict order of precedence to the Sheldonian Theatre. In Brasenose I was introduced as the new or newish Professor of Poetry to the Chancellor, Harold Macmillan, as he then was, distinguished in his black and gold. Plainly he had not heard of my ratting on the duty of delivering the oration, for he told me, in our brief conversation, as though to someone whose habits would naturally be rather better, that in his old age he read no Greek, but every day perused a page or two of Latin. It was probably at a later Encaenia, when he was much worse on his feet, that one heard he had refused some conveyance, perhaps a litter, to get him at the head of the procession to the Sheldonian: progress through the Oxford streets was snail-like but triumphant. This must have been about the time he was entertained to lunch by the BBC Board of Governors. When the moment came for him to say the customary few words afterwards, to open a discussion, the bowed, rather collapsed figure, giving the impression of being not far from the end, rose to its feet (such guests usually remaining seated), miraculously filled out, and delivered a trenchant and witty wide-ranging homily.

It was not until September 1971 that I heard from Sir Folliott again about the oration. Council had agreed that it might henceforth be delivered in English, and the necessary legisla-

tion was being promoted. This was duly given effect, and it fell
to me to deliver the oration at the 1972 Encaenia. Sir Folliott
supplied me with material about University events, honours,
distinctions and benefactions during the year, and when I sent
him the draft started his letter of acknowledgement (full of
excellent comment and suggestions): 'If I may say so, I was
quite delighted with your oration. It seems to me that you have
got both the tone and what nowadays is regrettably called the
"mix" exactly right; and the speech is certainly not too long to
be delivered in full.' I was pleased about this, for I had tried to
enliven the pedestrian listings with the literary allusions and
facetiousness evidently traditional, and to which a dead
language gave an inimitable flavour. He had warned me about
possible cuts: that there were to be none was further evidence of
success. (I print part of the oration in an appendix.)

Sir Folliott also sent me fool-proof procedural notes as to how
I was to get from my place in the procession to my seat in the
eyrie in the Sheldonian from which at the due time I was to
orate, and when to doff my cap to the Chancellor, and so forth.
The only thing missing was a glass of water. Nerves and Lord
Crewe's champagne had made me dry, and whether my mild
witticisms were any clearer than if uttered in Latin, *quaere*.

3

Such is Oxford's prestige, the title of 'Professor', fortuitously
acquired for five years, lingers on to this day. I never much liked
to employ it myself even in office, and when I joined the Board
of Governors of the BBC in 1972, the end of my Oxford career
in sight (my last lecture was during the 1972 Michaelmas term),
I asked the Director-General's office not to use the handle. It
was too late: labels with 'Professor' had been printed to stick on
the great envelopes full of bumf that were to arrive for the next
seven or so years. Besides, I think the BBC found it difficult to
believe that anyone appointed to the Board might be a plain
'Mr'.

I suppose I solved the problems of the Oxford professorship
as well as most outsiders. I was helped by the presence there of

my son and his family, and the fact that not long after election I
gave up my full-time lawyer's job. Cecil Day Lewis sometimes
took a railway day-return ticket to deliver his termly lecture,
and one cannot blame him, having regard to the stipend paid. I
was occasionally asked what I would do to improve the useful-
ness of the office – poet in residence the sort of thing suggested,
the stipend perhaps augmented by the Arts Council. Certainly
now, I think the office well left alone; a curious anomaly,
typically English. Anyone desiring it, or willing to stand, will
have his reasons – duty, publicity, discoveries to impart – and
will contribute, however strangely, to the long history of the
chair.

Without the spur of the office I would never have produced a
single, let alone two, books of criticism. Some of the things in
Owls and Artificers and *Professors and Gods* I am glad to have
perpetuated in print, perhaps especially the business about
syllabic verse in a lecture called 'An Artifice of Versification'. As
I wrote in a postscript to the lecture, part of it derived from an
already extant lecture and review. When in 1969 I was rearrang-
ing and adding to this material I was conscious of Elizabeth
Daryush as a poet who had used syllabics, but merely mentioned her as such. Then, as the time for the delivery of the
lecture approached, I was seized with guilt at not having
investigated her further. She had been born, a daughter of
Robert Bridges, the year before my mother, in 1887 – early
enough for her arrival to have been commented on by Gerard
Manley Hopkins – so was then aged eighty-two. I was uncertain
whether she would be willing to suffer, or be capable of
responding to, an enquiry from a stranger about verse technique – perhaps, indeed, whether or not she was still in the land
of the living – accordingly, I wrote to the second Lord Bridges
(Robert's grandson), who had just succeeded his father to the
barony, probably addressing my letter to the House of Lords,
for I was not acquainted with him. I received an encouraging
reply, so I wrote to Mrs Daryush at Stockwell, Boars Hill,
Oxford, where Lord Bridges said she was still living. I trust it
will be of interest to reproduce that first exchange of letters in
October 1969.

Dear Mrs Daryush,

I hope you will forgive me for troubling you with this letter. As the current Oxford Professor of Poetry I am lecturing on 6 November about syllabic verse. I was led to the subject by a talk I gave some time ago to the Royal Society of Literature about my own experience of the metre and a review of Marianne Moore's *Collected Poems* I did for *The Times Literary Supplement*. I'm not an academic and I don't really think of myself as a critic, but for the forthcoming lecture I was led deeper into the subject than I'd been before. In my first draft of the lecture I merely mentioned you as one of the poets of our time who have experimented with syllabic counts, but then I felt guilty at not having made a more thorough investigation. I have to confess that at that moment I thought your experiments were mainly confined to combining a regular syllabic count with regular stress. But from your note to *The Last Man* I have been led to *Verses, Fourth Book* – and then, of course, to a closer look at your poetry and the belated realization that it often embodies 'true' syllabic practice. I've now revised the lecture in several places and hope I've done justice to the clear and penetrating things you said about syllabics in the Thirties. The point of this letter is to ask you two things:

1. I guess in my lecture that your syllabics were inspired by your father's investigations into Milton's blank verse and his own experiments in classical metres. Is this a fair statement?
2. I say that I haven't been able to discover any overt links between you and Miss Moore. Were you ever in communication; and did you know her work before your own experiments; and if so, were you influenced by it?

Please do not bother to reply to this if it is a burden, though I think your answers would illuminate an obscure bit of literary history! I've been greatly impressed with everything you say about syllabics: you have confirmed, with greater precision, the opinions I'd formed about several practical points in which I differ from Miss Moore.

Two things embarrass me now about this letter: the underlying assumption that someone in her eighties might be gaga or at least have lost interest in art; and its referring to a considerable corpus of verse as 'experimental'. But Mrs Daryrush

promptly and fully replied. I may say that despite its reference
to her sight, the letter is written with a steel nib in an italic hand
reminiscent, if lacking the full beauty, of her father's – a fine
specimen of which I was to see by chance a few years later when
as a governor of the BBC I visited its written archive, where
among other literary treasures had been laid out for my inspection a holograph script of a Robert Bridges's radio talk.

Dear Mr Fuller,
    Many thanks for your letter. In answer to your first question:
it is hardly correct to say that my syllabic ventures were 'inspired
by' my father's 'investigations into Milton's blank verse, and his
own experiments in classical metres'. I now realise that my
inclination towards this form goes back a very long way. In my
second collection (1916) a distinctly childish production which
I have since suppressed, there are obvious signs of it. I remember my father asking me, with regard to a piece in this book
which he particularly liked, 'What is this new metre?' and my
reply of 'only syllables'. (But perhaps you need not repeat this in
your lecture.) However, my approach, in direct contrast to his
own, has never been deliberately technical. What rules I have
arrived at are the result of an often almost unconscious analysis
of my dissatisfaction, or otherwise, with what I have already
(again half sub-consciously) written. And despite his often
expressed opinion, by which I have no doubt been influenced,
that the traditional 'accentual syllabics' were, as he put it,
'played out', and his life-long interest in technical possibilities, I
think that perhaps he never quite appreciated the full implication of a whole-hearted surrender to the syllabic principle – as,
for instance, in the use of unaccented rhymes, and the strict
avoidance of all ambiguity in the matter of elision.
    Owing to failing eyesight, my knowledge of modern verse is
minimal – Marianne Moore is little more than a name to me –
apart from one or two casual perusals in anthologies I know
nothing of her work.
    If at any time you should be in Oxford and would care to visit
me here, it would be a great pleasure to meet you, and to discuss
these matters at greater length than is possible in a letter. I have
some recent, unpublished work, which might possibly be of
interest to you.

I took up Mrs Daryush's invitation when I went to Oxford to deliver my lecture of that Trinity Term, 'An Artifice of Versification'. 'Stockwell', as she precisely told me in a further letter, was the last house 'on the Ridgeway on the left. To find the Ridgeway you go first to Ripon Hall, a castle-like place on the top of Boar's Hill – and take the middle road of the cross-roads just after it.'

I had never before been to Boar's Hill, and at Stockwell (somehow prefigured by the Daryushes' pink-printed, private-pressy writing-paper) found myself in the vanished world of Bridges, Masefield, the young Robert Graves – a large house but rather spartan; a courteous reception from the owners; provision of good coffee; literary talk. I came away with the MS of her new book of poems! She had once been published by the Oxford University Press, but they had abandoned her in the late Thirties, and she had brought out her last book privately. I knew Jon Stallworthy quite well, who was then working for the Press, and I approached him to ask if there was any hope of their taking her on again. He was not sanguine, though sportingly read the MS (Mrs Daryush had offered to get it typed, but because of her eyesight it would have taken some time to correct the resulting typescript).

Jon's verdict was adverse, but in the end Michael Schmidt of the Carcanet Press brought the book out. Those were the days when Carcanet was run more modestly than now, from Pin Farm, a rural setting difficult to get to by car, entangled as it was by main roads on the outskirts of Oxford. But even then Michael was practical and enthusiastic about bringing into print (or back into print) the unfashionable (as well as promoting new authors), though one had no conception of the substantial and remarkable publisher he would become. About what was called, with typical austerity, *Verses Seventh Book*, he wrote to me: 'The Daryush goes to press today . . . I have read the book closely now, and can say frankly that I don't like it at all! But I see the point of publishing it as an historical piece more than anything else.' However, he went on to publish a *Selected Poems* in 1972, and a *Collected Poems* in 1976, the latter with an introduction by Donald Davie, far more comprehensive than the similar office I had performed for *Verses Seventh Book*. Michael also visited and made friends with the Daryushes: I never myself went back, though Mrs Daryush had issued an open invitation – my usual combination of diffidence and failure of duty (however dutiful in some areas I might appear). But I did in 1970 put her in touch with the *Southern Review*, the great literary quarterly from Louisiana State University, where at that time Professor Donald E. Stanford was an editor; and poetry of hers appeared there – three of her last poems after her death in her ninetieth year on 7 April 1977. I knew Don would be sympathetic – as his mentor Yvor Winters had been in the Thirties – not only because of his expertise in English prosody but also because he was then in the process of becoming the leading authority on Robert Bridges and the Bridges circle; it being left to him by unenterprising English academics to bring out an edition of Bridges's letters. It may also be added that the disloyalty of the marooning of Elizabeth Daryush by the OUP in the Thirties is only exceeded by their allowing the *Poetical Works* of her father in the Oxford Standard Authors series to go out of print in the Eighties.

Mr Daryush, though not in good health at the time of my visit, lived on to a great age. It was a surprise (though the Laureate had described him in a letter of 2 November 1923 as 'a very excellent and solid person') that when the amount of his estate was published in *The Times* on 22 June 1989, it well exceeded a million pounds. I thought at once of the development value of the house and garden on the Ridgeway, but Don Stanford told me, perhaps more plausibly, that the then Lord Bridges, the poet's great-grandson, thought Mr Daryush had secretly been playing the stock market, an activity his wife would have disapproved of. The money went to the Oxford Preservation Trust; most appropriate destination, though one wishes some of it could have been used to keep Elizabeth's and her father's work in print. When I wrote to Mr Daryush after his wife's death, he said that of all the letters he had received mine gave him the greatest condolence. I think I had simply said what I believe to be true, that any account of the century's poetry would have to take notice of his wife's work.

V

BOG

I

Towards the end of 1971 I received, out of the blue, a letter from Christopher Chataway, then Minister for Posts and Telecommunications, inviting me to become a member of the Board of Governors of the BBC on 1 January 1972. I was flattered, had no hesitation in accepting, and was able to do so because the BBC Governors met on Thursdays, the Woolwich Board on Tuesdays. In due course I had a letter from Lord Hill of Luton, the then Chairman of the BBC, asking me to arrange to call and see him at Broadcasting House, in advance of the first governors' meeting in 1972, so that he could provide an initiation. However, before the date of the appointment arrived, I was telephoned one morning by Colin Shaw, the BBC Secretary, to ask if I could attend an emergency meeting at BH that very afternoon. A car would be sent for me (my first experience of what proved a vital element in my BBC service: the Director-General's office once told me, not entirely jocularly, that sorting out governors' transport was their heaviest burden). The sudden crisis had arisen because the Government was putting pressure on the Corporation to withdraw a television programme called 'The Question of Ulster'. The programme was to be live, open-ended, and give all parties in Northern Ireland the opportunity to put their case. It was the platform the programme would incidentally give to the extremists that had drawn the Government's fire. For my part, I went to the meeting ready to go to the Tower, so to speak, for the right to proceed with the programme, which from all I had heard seemed balanced and sensible, and more likely to do good than otherwise.

A fair muster of governors had been assembled in the quite small Boardroom in the modest gubernatorial suite at BH which was to become so familiar. Lord Hill was in the Chair, with the Director-General, Charles Curran, himself from the Province, on his right, and a sprinkling of executives, all to become (like the suite) closely known in the ensuing years. I heard it said that the BBC was an enterprise as big as Vauxhall Motors, but of course its proportion of officers to troops must be vastly higher. In fact, in my experience I doubt if any British organization, including universities and the Civil Service, contained a greater percentage of able brains and fluent tongues. Charles Curran may stand for many. Before joining BOG I had read that Charles, then quite a new DG (succeeding the charismatic Hugh Carleton Greene) was a rather faceless 'corporation man'. However, I soon found it apparent that his grasp of the Corporation's affairs, and knowledge of its personnel, was wide and profound – facts, figures and assessments rising rapidly to the surface of his capacious memory and brain. One could well understand his being chosen by BOG for the job in preference to more superficially glamorous candidates. At the emergency meeting he defended the projected programme, but I think no voice was really heard against it. The Government had a constitutional right to forbid it, but we decided to call its bluff (the situation has been repeated in recent times, but then was far from stereotyped). There was one snag. The leading representative of one of the Northern Ireland political parties due to appear had been prevented for some reason: no plausible substitute was available or willing. But some lowly member of the party in question, long eager to distinguish himself on the box or otherwise, had been unearthed by BBC Belfast. It was decided that his appearance would satisfy the criterion of 'balance'. The Government kept mum, the worthy programme went out: the post mortem proved that though viewers may have been bored, few or none were offended.

I never kept my preliminary appointment with Lord Hill: I said or wrote to him that I thought the emergency meeting was sufficient introduction to the *mores* of BOG. Soon, I fell into the routine of the fortnightly BOG meetings, alternating between Broadcasting House and Television Centre. Committee meetings and other engagements (some to try to get to know parts of the far-flung BBC empire), and a phenomenal amount of received paper, extended the time spent on BBC business, which was then rewarded on a meagre scale, later somewhat improved. I never grudged the amount of work I put in. If I may say so, I was an ideal governor: familiar with the arts; liking discriminatingly a good few popular entertainments, such as jazz and stand-up comedians; experienced in the law and the workings of a large corporation; and with a fair knowledge of the world of real property. One example will suffice: when I joined BOG the BBC was in the throes of quite complicated property transactions to do with TV Centre at Shepherd's Bush, and surrounding sites. It was plain to me that the inevitable expansion of the BBC should be there, and that Broadcasting House and the expensive or valuable overflow premises nearby ought eventually to consist merely of a West End presence. A fair time after I had left BOG this was being brought to fulfilment following some side-slipping.

As in the case of Charles Curran, Lord Hill's reputation had unfairly preceded my knowing him. He had been Chairman of the Independent Television Authority, and it was generally said that his appointment to his present position was Harold Wilson's way of dotting the eye of the BBC, which he conceived never gave him or his party fair do's. Previously, Charles Hill had of course been the celebrated, even notorious, 'Radio Doctor'; Secretary to the British Medical Association during its duel with Aneurin Bevan over National Health; and then, as a nominally curious 'Liberal and Conservative', a member of the House of Commons, and holder of several Ministerial posts. I had once in the past seen him in the flesh when he spoke at a Building Societies Institute dinner (no doubt in 1961 or '62 when he was Minister for Housing and Local Government): my memory of that occasion was of him taking a long swallow of a glass of lager at the bar after dinner.

But right from the start all these aliases and activities, some, possibly all, of which might have been thought dubious by an intellectual, were replaced by the man himself, whom I got to know well, even in the short time remaining of his office as BBC Chairman (and also thereafter). He was a truly excellent Chairman of a committee; providing a warm atmosphere; letting everyone have his say before bringing a matter to a decision, yet getting expeditiously through the agenda. Naturally, he wanted his own way, but when he realized he was not going to get it accepted the fact with good humour. His previous career had accustomed him to 'politicking', but his manoeuvres in that regard were usually transparent – 'Most openly devious of men' I described him in a set of couplets I read at the farewell dinner for his successor but one, George Howard. He himself was a masterly after-dinner speaker, with the timing of an expert comedian, only falling down somewhat when he very occasionally broke into what had evidently been his hustings style of conventional rhetoric.

His character may be measured by his affection for, and the affection he inspired in, his wife Marion. Like the Rostrevor Hamiltons, theirs was a life-long love affair. Quite early in the days of my knowing them, Marion's health, indeed life, was threatened, but treatment was successful, and she happily survived. Charles had, of course, practised as a doctor in former times, and the question of Marion's health accordingly weighed all the more heavily on him. Clinical medicine lost a good practitioner when he moved into administration and politics (the same, so I was told by his former boss at St Thomas's Hospital, applies to Dr David Owen). I was much impressed when, during BOG interviews for a BBC post, Charles was against one candidate on the grounds that he was liable, from his looks, to coronary thrombosis – even more impressed when the chap subsequently had one. As I remarked at the time, Charles had added a fresh terror to job interviews.

The foregoing sketch of Charles was written before his death on 22 August 1989. I wondered how Marion would take it. He had once said to me that neither of them 'wished to be the first to go'. On Friday, 17 November 1989, I went to his memorial service in Westminster Abbey. Before proceedings started, one of the officiating clergy announced that Marion had died the previous Tuesday. It was a shock, but, reflecting during the hymns and prayers and tributes – words and tunes from the remoteness of one's schooldays – one felt Charles's wish had been refused in a merciful way. At the buffet lunch afterwards in the Cholmondeley Room in the House of Lords, Roger Cary, the BBC's great man of protocol, told me that Marion had planned to come to the service in a wheelchair. She was eighty-six.

Charles Hill's relationship with Charles Curran would have served as a strand of a novel by C. P. Snow. BOG met over coffee, informally in an anteroom, without the three officials (DG, Secretary and Assistant Secretary) who attended the formal meetings, for the half hour (9 to 9.30 am) before their start. In early days governors simply drifted in in penny numbers, and until Charles Hill arrived the conversation might well be mainly personal. But Charles would almost always have some internal or external crux to ventilate, or scandal to impart, and there would be some useful off-the-record beefing. Quite soon, most governors turned up for the full preliminary half hour, and when Michael Swann succeeded Charles this became *de rigueur*. Charles Hill's usual burden *vis-à-vis* Charles Curran was that the latter would not be decisive enough off his own bat, though consistently encouraged by the other Charles. I daresay Charles Curran would have told a different story. Personally, I believed that Charles Hill did not hog the decision-making process, and that Charles Curran lacked a clinching confidence. But really the two worked effectively together in practice, whatever their criticism of each other, and I would be the last to reproach Charles Curran for relying on Charles Hill in some difficult areas. One incident, however, showed me both sides, rather to Charles Curran's advantage, though I think it was not typical.

Charles Curran certainly overworked himself; that may have contributed to his hesitancy about decisions. Charles Hill wanted him to ease his burden by letting BOG appoint a Deputy Director-General. In this notion he probably had the support of the majority of governors: certainly I liked the idea. Charles Curran himself was so much against it that he approached governors in confidence, individually and privately, to drive his arguments home. One governor (I never knew his identity) leaked this action to Charles Hill. In his turn, Charles Hill asked each governor separately if the aforesaid approach had been made to him or her. It was an awkward situation. Like George Washington, I could not tell a lie. Besides, thinking on the spot, I realized if I were caught out in a lie my relations with Charles Hill (whom I was growing fond of) would have been greatly damaged. In the end the appointment was not made, and the matter proved to be only fleetingly important – except that I felt a seed of unease had been planted between myself and Charles Curran. So some five years later, just before he retired, I wrote to him, confessing my betrayal of his confidence (by then Charles Hill had long ceased to be Chairman). In his letter of reply he revealed that he had known, through Tom Jackson, of Charles Hill's member by member interrogation of BOG. It seems that Tom was the only governor 'sufficiently political' (in Charles Curran's phrase) to deny the confidential approach, although he was one of the first to whom the approach was made. Charles Curran was generous about my (then historical) dilemma, and said that behind the proposed appointment was Charles Hill's desire to confer the succession to DG on Ian Trethowan by engineering his appointment as Deputy. This outcome was, as will be seen, achieved without intrigue.

The committee of executives corresponding to the gubernatorial BOG was BOM, the Board of Management. When I arrived, BOM was still holding out on its stiff-necked position that its minutes should not be seen by BOG, though the stance was soon abandoned under pressure, and the minutes added to BOG's bumf. There was a healthy opposition between BOG and BOM, more acute than I had experienced between analogous groups in the Woolwich, simply because of the greater scope and intellectual power involved, and also because of the extent and intensity of the interest taken by BOG in the BBC. It is a fact, though a cliché, to say that the BBC *is* the Board of Governors, in the sense that BOG represents the licence-holders (theoretically virtually the whole population), and carries the responsibility (finally, to the Government of the day) for the BBC's activities. The conflict took many forms, in many areas, though further down the executive line BOG would often be seen merely as a bunch of fuddy-duddies trying (*inter alia*) to suppress freedom of expression. Yet I believe without doubt – certainly during my time – that the organization 'worked', though certainly depending on a strong, conscientious BOG. I found that one of the prime duties of BOG was to try to make more reasonable the almost pathological defensiveness of the BBC, which sometimes manifested itself in retaining in their place (even promoting) personnel who had gravely boobed; and repeating (often in the programme area) the offences that had led to legitimate attacks. Of course, the BBC is constantly under fire from politicians and other philistines, so its extreme defensiveness is explicable.

As in all British institutions, the troops are more or less bolshie *vis-à-vis* the top brass. That is why it is essential for the top brass to be aware how they look from below, and above all not to try to curry favour from the potentially disaffected. A small example of the dangers and disagreeableness in this relationship arose during my governorship when I was asked by Humphrey Burton, then Head of TV Music and Arts, to address a meeting of producers and their staff in his department. The idea was to say a few words about the gubernatorial role, and then answer questions. Why on earth did I agree to perform this task, which I see clearly now as a heads they win, tails I lose situation, and also one I could have decently evaded? Details of what actually occurred have mercifully been expunged from memory, but I think the questioning mainly concerned an act or acts of so-called censorship approved of, or even possibly imposed, by BOG. The session from my point of view was deeply unsuccessful – something I am not used to, for, not to boast unduly, I am quite a good trooper, normally giving decent value. But the format, as well as the select audience, was wrong. However, the worst part of the proceedings came towards the end of my performance, with the entry, to a buzz of interest, of Dennis Potter and his producer, Ken Loach (or perhaps Tony Garnett). They were to follow me in the hot seat. Though I had another engagement later, I had a little time to spare, and thought it would be courteous to stay on a while. I hoisted myself on a table behind the two new speakers, and in this informal posture – somewhat ingratiatingly informal, I afterwards felt – listened to part of a session of marked contrast to the one I had just conducted.

Dennis Potter was already, through his physical disability and 'challenging' TV drama, a famous figure much approved of by the broad left. Indeed, it may well have been that the higher editorial quashing of his play about the seduction of a handicapped girl had just taken place, and was the reason behind his and my appearance. His reception by the assembled staff was like that of a well-loved comic; his least observation received with warmth, often with laughter. I sat the thing out until I had to leave to keep my date, but the management of my face involved some play-acting, also retrospectively deplored.

Middlebrow, but sexually and (to an extent) politically probing the limits of programming, Dennis Potter's art is regarded as high art within television. So much tripe is purveyed by the medium that this attitude seems plausible to many outside.

BOG was a typically British institution; in some almost mystical way democratic and unauthoritarian. Its members are appointed by the Government, which has often been accused of political prejudice in its choice. I can only say that I never recall the governors, collectively or individually, taking a decision on party political grounds. When German television made a film about the BBC, they were astonished that the governors were not elected or other delegates of organizational interests, and that they sat round the Board table in haphazard and ever-shifting places. Actually, there was always one appointment which in practice was political – the trade union governor, of which there were three in my time: Tom Jackson, Vic Feather and Alf Allen. Perhaps it is worth saying something about how these appointees fitted in.

Tom Jackson, the TU man when I joined, was a familiar ikon – his large moustache, side-whiskers, and rotund countenance, had not long before constantly appeared on TV screens during a Union of Post Office Workers' (as it then was) extended strike. He was still General Secretary of his union, so that his gov-

ernorship was very much a sideline – but his active involvement
in social questions and political events ensured acuteness and
relevance in his contributions to BOG. The bluff, humorous,
Yorkshire exterior concealed something of an intellectual: in his
retirement he became an antiquarian bookseller in his native
county, specializing in cookery books and patronized in that
capacity by my brother, a devoted collector.

Tom was succeeded by Vic Feather, another Yorkshireman,
immensely celebrated as the General Secretary of the TUC
(from which he had recently retired), and subsequently ennobled. He was appointed to rather too many bodies, and I
think it is fair to say that the best of him was not seen at the
BBC. But on questions of tactics, where politicians, civil
servants or the public at large were concerned, he was masterly,
and of course he, too, was no slouch intellectually, especially in
matters of art. And so far as the broad masses were concerned,
he must have been a reassuring figure on BOG. I remember
coming back from a visit by BOG to some outpost of the BBC
(regularly undertaken), and walking with Vic along a platform
at Paddington towards the barrier. It was like the progress of
some democratic monarch – respectful but familiar salutations
from every species of railway worker, and from not a few
bystanders.

I guess Vic had once been a cigarette smoker, turned to cigars
after the lung-cancer scare – and cigars not of the miniature
variety nor even cheroots, but formidable objects which it quite
hurt me to see him puffing on his arrival early in the day for
meetings of BOG. I was still sensitive about smoking, having
myself given up a career of cigarettes on 1 April 1972 without
taking to a substitute. Vic had the characteristic 'chestiness' of
the working man getting on in years, and indeed, soon after he
came on BOG, had the experience (immediately turned into a
comic fatalistic anecdote) of being diagnosed as possessing, and
X-rayed for, suspicious heart or lungs (which organ, and the
result, he left his listeners in doubt about, in true TU official
style). But he seemed to have won through all this until one
night he excused himself in the middle of a BOG dinner in the
governors' suite in BH. When he had left, Denis Greenhill, a

fellow governor, caught my eye, and we both followed Vic into the lavatory in the corridor opposite. By the time we got there Vic had loosened his collar and more or less recovered from whatever 'turn' had overcome him. I remember thinking how many of the desperate crises of life occur in lavatories, the death of Evelyn Waugh an example.

Vic (his wife, too) was always a pleasure to be with: no side, but on the other hand, no false pastoral. My wife, who likes to raise such subjects, sat next to him at a BBC dinner, and asked him about life after death. 'There's nowt, love,' he said. Lady Feather once disclosed that she was quite liberal with water in her making of Yorkshire pudding, another controversial topic of Kate's interest.

On Vic's death the Government may have had some difficulty in filling the trade union place, for there was quite a hiatus before the appointment of Alf Allen. He arrived for the first time one evening when the governors were dining together at BH, having just completed the exhausting business of appointing a new Director General to succeed Charles Curran. We had interviewed several distinguished outside candidates as well as the internal probables. At the end of that process as, awash with coffee, we looked at one another round the Board table (a far more modest affair than the horse-shoe at Equitable House), I had a brainwave, and proposed that without more ado we ruled out all the external interviewees. After a brief, possibly half-stunned silence, the proposal was accepted, and a great deal of discussion avoided. The course of the interviews had confirmed my ideological preconception that the DG should come from within, and have been a programme maker or performer.

The power of the BBC governors resides mainly in three areas. Most important is the reservation (in my time, anyway) of appointing all staff of the rank of Controller and upward, and taking a close interest in, wanting to be warned about, the appointment of other key staff, such as the editor of the *Listener* (when that paper was still the BBC's intellectual organ). Less spectacular is the close involvement in financial and property matters. Finally, I believe that BOG's keen interest in programmes ('Programme Comment' was an item that appeared on every fortnightly agenda) had an effect, even if seemingly that of water dripping on a stone. Of course, other factors played a part; not least the personality and assiduity of individual governors, and the ability of the Chairman in his relations with both his colleagues and the staff, and his strength and tact with politicians – usually antagonistic and sometimes meddlesome.

Charles Hill was followed by another outstanding Chairman, Michael Swann. In my eyes it was a severe test when he first turned up to take a Board meeting, so stimulating and genial had been Charles Hill. But by his second Board meeting he had passed with honours. As Vice-Chancellor of Edinburgh University he had also come successfully through the epoch of revolting students: in appointing him to the BBC (Michael said), Edward Heath told him he thought of it as resembling a university – a shrewd observation: clever, though not always sound, dons; clever, though often unruly, rank and file. Incidentally, by the time I joined BOG, Labour's high dudgeon over the programme 'Yesterday's Men' had cooled down. Harold Wilson was one of the first guests in my day that BOG entertained, and asked to start a discussion, at one of its fortnightly lunches: when he had gone it was said he had buried the hatchet – but marked the spot.

To return to the arrival of Alf Allen among the ranks of the governors – that evening he was greeted by the news that the new DG had just been decided on. It was Ian Trethowan. No choice among the candidates could have more aroused Alf's suspicions – that the appointment was a right-wing plot, and that it had been hastened to deny Alf a say in it. I am deducing the black-and-whiteness of his emotions, but there is no doubt that on that evening, and for some time thereafter, Alf behaved very cagily. I suppose the governors' euphoria over pre-prandial drinks at the end of two taxing days of interviews did not improve Alf's state of mind.

Alf was still General Secretary of the Union of Shop, Distributive and Allied Workers, which had its headquarters in Manchester, though himself was from Bristol and had retained his West Country burr. He had recently been ennobled as Lord Allen of Fallowfield, the district of Manchester where he lived, familiar from my boyhood and giving me a talking point with him. He was a tall, stately man; no doubt also once a cigarette smoker, he had gone over, like Vic, to cigars. I liked him, and his wife, and quite soon he unbent a bit, revealed a subtle sense of humour, and (in the tradition of Tom and Vic) was invaluable on social and political problems. It was a bonus that (again like his predecessors) he was a man of culture. He died at too early an age.

There is also a tradition that BOG shall include a retired diplomat. When I arrived Sir Ralph Murry occupied that slot, able and conscientious; no slouch, if no vivid personality. He was succeeded by Sir Denis (now Lord) Greenhill, then lately Head of the Diplomatic Service. Like Vic, his retirement had been followed by appointments to numerous bodies, including the Board of the sickly British Leyland Motor Corporation. But he was undaunted by his assortment of hats, and played a strong character part on BOG – as he had in diplomatic fancy dress in the pioneering BBC film about the Royal family. He was – is – a calm, handsome man who, though a product of Christ Church, had had by no means an orthodox diplomatic beginning, for he had not entered the service until after the war, when he was demobilized with the rank of Colonel in his early thirties.

I liked making jokes round the Board table, but Denis trumped not a few of my aces. He also had an apt vocabulary: '*vieux chapeau*' about some propounded idea; 'of course, he'll leave with a bag of gold' about some departing figure in the commercial world. From his lips I first heard the phrase 'slush fund'. He brought to BOG a healthy impatience, even cynicism, about the BBC, though properly defensive when it mattered, particularly as to the perennially cheeseparing attitude of the FCO to the BBC External Services. I suppose I myself was too sentimental about the Corporation. Like Edward Heath, I thought of it as a university, a university open to all; an island of culture in the very areas where philistinism might be especially rampant. To justify the licence fee it had to capture an audience, but one closed an ear to, say, Radio 1, and believed (theoretically, at any rate) in the ameliorative power of the services in general. Reithian notions prevailed, not only in one's own mind but also in the minds of most, if not all, senior executives – though faith occasionally languished, strangely enough, it was sustained not least by refugees from European tyranny, Stephen Hearst and George Fischer (though there were others of similar calibre, British born, such as Jim Norris, the Assistant Secretary, whose minutes of BOG meetings were works of intellect and wit).

It is curious that despite the quality of staff, even in my time a war had to be waged against degenerating standards in speech and decorum in BBC programmes. The bug was already biting of the denial that such standards could exist; and editorial control was being christened 'censorship'. I wonder if one's objections as a governor had any effect. I suppose it is just possible that the mispronunciations, wrong emphases, constant vulgar innuendoes, spread of 'pop' music, that have multiplied during the decade since I left BOG, might have occurred earlier in the absence of gubernatorial protest. As to pronunciation, I cannot believe that in the Seventies educated people, as they do now – even those employed as readers and presenters in broad-casting – omitted essential 'ts' and inserted redundant 'ts' (go' i' for got it, tha' for that – the latter an example from an actor in the National Theatre Company; Tot-tenham, Sut-ton, settul and battul for settle and battle); said zoology as though the first syllable were a place for captive animals; missed out the 'g' sound in words like strength; emphasized the adjectival part of a phrase, regardless of sense, when reading from a text (*Secret* Service, *festive* season, blown from their beds by a *massive* explosion); or *vice versa* (drug *pushers*, stamp *dealers*); substi-tuted 'rs' for 'ws' – ror eggs (an example by David Frost, though common); used the American pronunciation of 'schedule'. Producers of programmes seem to be unaware that the BBC has a pronunciation unit. Nor can I believe that in those former days fashionable words and phrases infected the patter of BBC employees and fee-takers as well as that of laymen – brilliant; at the end of the day; bottom line; if you like; it's as simple as that; I have to say; the fact of the matter is; basically: as I write, these can be heard scores of times a week. And surely 'humour' was not so vulgar, even outrageous, as now; studio audiences so ready, so encouraged to pick up sexual *double entendres*. I rarely watch such programmes on TV, yet during the last year or two I have overheard 'jokes' about colostomy bags, a monstrous breach of taste and compassion.

When I joined BOG the recommendations of the internal paper, *Broadcasting in the Seventies*, had already taken effect in radio. It was a paper I should have opposed had I been on the scene, for it led to ghettoization, a neglect of Reithian principles. At one end of the spectrum was the frightful Radio 1, at the other the virtual disappearance of the highbrow spoken element, for which more or less continuous serious music on Radio 3 was no substitute. A decade after I had left two small incidents occurred which I felt illustrated further slackening of intellectual grip.

One day at the counter of the London Library an elderly man at my side asked me, apropos of the book I was returning, if it mentioned Balfour Gardiner, British composer not unknown before the First World War. In typically gormless manner, off guard, I made some equivocal answer. The exchange was amiable but brief: when my *vis-à-vis* had departed I enquired his name of the staff member at the counter. 'Sir Thomas Armstrong.' Of course, I knew precisely who he was – composer, organist, ex-principal of the Royal College of Music. And simultaneously, to my chagrin, I remembered that the book in question had contained quite a few things about Balfour Gardiner. I felt I had to write to Sir Thomas to put the record straight, so I found his address in *Who's Who*, and we exchanged letters.

Some time later than this, in 1985 in fact, in Peter Heyworth's excellent *Conversations with Klemperer*, I came across the name Ivan Knorr, I think for the first time. At any rate, it inspired a sonnet, into which I also brought the encounter with Tom Armstrong, for Knorr had been the father of the so-called 'Frankfurt School', among which had been numbered, as well as Cyril Scott, Roger Quilter, Norman O'Neill *et al*, Balfour Gardiner:

> Knorr's packet soup . . . I think of Ivan Knorr,
> The teacher of the English 'Frankfurt School' –

Quilter and Scott and Balfour Gardiner.
Who plays them now? Yet not very long ago,
At the counter of the London Library,
Through a strange mix of circumstance, I spoke
Of long-dead Balfour Gardiner with one
Who knew him and his worth. Undoubtedly
Much music lies inertly on the page
(That page an unlucky courtier out of favour)
Though capable, like vegetable soup
In powdered form, if treated (so to speak)
According to the directions on the pack,
Of burgeoning to near-fresh hues and flavour.

I dedicated this piece to 'Sir Thomas Armstrong', and sent
him a copy; shortly thereafter I finished the little sequence I
called 'Kitchen Sonnets' and also sent him a copy of *PN Review*
in which the sequence first appeared. We thus had another
exchange of letters. Everything he wrote – in an elegant italic-
influenced, steel-nibbed hand that reminded me of Elizabeth
Daryush's (even his writing-paper, pinkish printed address,
resembled hers) – was of interest, not least about Balfour
Gardiner, who formed a sort of ground-bass to our correspondence, and whose excellent biography by Stephen Lloyd I had
at last extracted from the London Library, some member
having evidently sat on it from the time Tom had first recommended it to me. Well in advance of Tom's ninetieth birthday
on 15 June 1988, I wrote to Radio 3, suggesting that it be
celebrated by playing some of his music. To my fury that was
not done.

I was a bit less annoyed with Radio 3 over the centenary of
Arthur Waley's birth on 19 August 1989, for in that connection
I felt my own interest was being advanced. His widow was keen
that it should be marked by the playing of an interview I
conducted with Waley for the Third Programme in 1963. I say
'interview', but in fact there were two. At that period I had done
several programmes with a Third Programme producer called
Helen Rapp; attractive, and highly intelligent and competent,
another of those BBC employees, of continental origin, who

sustained the Reithian tradition. At that time she was married to Georg Rapp, a metal tycoon, who round about then sold his business to devote himself to publishing (and perhaps writing) poetry. By an odd coincidence he was a fan of my verse, so I got to know him as well as his wife. Quite a few pages could be devoted to Georg's character and activities, but apart from two illustrative morsels I will stick to the matter in hand. Before he retired he had a beard: afterwards he shaved it off, revealing further sharp features; telling me that he felt it right to be a whiskered businessman but necessary to operate clean-shaven in the world of poetry. He also told me that in the course of some deal with Aston Martin he had stipulated that they supply him with one of their motor cars, adding 'Of course, at cost.' Aston Martin's managing director said: 'At cost you couldn't afford it' – illustrating, in a way, the fate of part of post-war British manufacturing industry.

I had brought the Waley undertaking on my own head. Over a post-recording drink with Helen in the Duty Officer's Room at Broadcasting House (a facility sometimes exploited near the embarrassing limit by other, notoriously boozy producers), I'd mentioned Waley as a fundamentally neglected poetic voice, and she immediately latched on to the notion of a programme about him as one of the century's originals, an interview rather than an illustrated talk, with me as interviewer, a role that at that date I don't think I'd ever assumed. Eventually the thing materialized, and I met Waley for the first time in Helen's office to talk matters briefly over. As we left for the studio, I asked him if he had seen a poem of mine addressed to him, published in 1955 in *The Listener*. 'Yes,' he said, 'you made me seem very old.' He added no further word. Though I saw at once the justice of his criticism – the poem had tried to patheticize things by rather prematurely adding age to undervaluation – I was chagrined.

I had done my homework, but in the studio it continued to be difficult to get Waley to enlarge on often telegraphese answers to questioning, though anything he actually uttered – about metrics, about dining with Pound and Eliot – was absorbing. In the end we had to call it a day (perhaps our studio time had run out), and a further session was arranged. Out of the two tapes, with the actor Gary Watson putting in some fine readings of the Chinese translations, Helen cunningly constructed a forty-minute programme of miraculous continuity and depth. A transcript was later published in the appreciation and anthology of Waley edited by Ivan Morris in 1970, *Madly Singing in the Mountains*. It was this programme that Alison Waley wanted broadcast, not only because it revealed Waley's greatness as a translator and part of the modern movement in English poetry, but also because through the rather high-pitched, rather harsh, Bloomsburian voice, it embodied the man, the personality.

The BBC had lost the tape. I told Alison I was sure I had once heard it had become part of the permanent archive. Still it did not turn up. She enlisted the help of Helen Rapp, by then retired from the BBC, and a copy was found in the British Library and lent to the BBC. They did not broadcast it – too long, too highbrow? – and the centenary day was marked by the repeat of what I felt to be an all-too-middlebrow biographical feature that had marked Waley's death in 1966.

However, when I was on BOG I believe in one area of decay I postponed the day of doom: I could not prevent Karl Miller resigning as editor of the *Listener* (and its eventual decline into middlebrowism) but I helped enure BOG to its loss-making existence. Perhaps in its present guise it does not make a loss.

The Oxford professorship, by bringing *Owls and Artificers* and *Professors and Gods* into being, somewhat assuaged my guilt at not turning out prose fiction. The BBC governorship, by providing a worthwhile occupation that filled some of the gaps in time outside my Woolwich directorship, was an equal alibi. I enjoyed the work more than any imposed work that had come my way, and I was extremely pleased when my five-years appointment was renewed for a further two and three-quarters. I even liked being picked up early at home on Board days – 7.45 to get there at 9.0 if the meeting was at TV Centre; 8.0 for Broadcasting House. The delays of the rush-hour seemed merely to make more tantalizing the coming pleasures of gossip, discussion and decisions among idiosyncratic friends. One got to know the BBC drivers, and even the drivers of the hire-cars sometimes provided, the resources of the BBC exhausted by governors' demands. All had their eccentric short-cuts (or, not infrequently, long-cuts, resulting from the professional driver's desire to keep on the move, and addiction to 'back doubles'), the BBC drivers usually proceeding to TV Centre, as Chesterton would have approved, *via* Balham; the latter being the magnetic headquarters of BBC transport. Tycoon-like, I sat in the rear seat, often with last-minute bumf spread out beside me, and with *The Times* if the newsagents had contrived to deliver it before departure. In the early and late summer the sun might beat on the back of my head as the journey west got under way, but the discomfort was somehow not disagreeable. Sometimes a quirk of traffic, or a driver's skill or good luck, would land me first in the anteroom at TV Centre or BH; occasionally, even before the arrival of the coffee-thermos and biscuits. Then the familiar figures would start to appear – an apostolic twelve if we were a full muster. With the entry of the Chairman the more formal gossip began, usually started by his retailing some internal development or political threat, governors probably getting the chance to voice any grouse they preferred to raise, initially at any rate, in the absence of the executive. At 9.30 we would move into the adjoining Boardroom, if at BH; at TV Centre we used a very plain room, tables pushed together, on the floor above, the sixth, that looked bleakly out over a flat roof.

One liked to make fresh jokes, but a few became hallowed. When the dormitory accommodation in the engineering training establishment at King's Norton was being enlarged, the specification and estimate prompted me to go on referring to it as the King's Norton Hilton. Behind the cosy facetiousness was a serious question: the BBC's traditional lavishness in not always appropriate areas – the 'brass handles syndrome', I seem to remember christening it. Like the Monarchy, the BBC sometimes perpetuated, or tried to perpetuate, a style admirable enough, but suited more to the days of Empire. Some might say the governors' transport fell into that category. Yet it was reassuring to have someone on tap like Roger Cary (second baronet and special assistant to the DG) for such things as Royal visits and retirement presents, with uninhibited notions of protocol and generosity. Like building societies, the BBC is an admirable *echt*-British creation which the rot of modern times does its best to ruin.

No doubt I was more than half in love with Auntie. I even quite enjoyed the quarterly meetings of the General Advisory Council. The GAC is a large appointed body, its members experts in their fields. At the cold buffet lunch before the quarterly meetings one might find oneself opposite Bishop (as he then was) Runcie, and between Alan Plater and Alan Beith, MP. The venue of the lunch was the ballroom of the former Langham Hotel, opposite BH, an establishment where before the war my brother had served as a wine waiter, part of his hotel training. The meetings themselves were held in the Council Chamber at the prow of BH, for most of my time chaired with panache by Lord Aldington. Here again was another odd link with the past, for Toby had once been Tory MP for Blackpool and a close friend of my wife's former boss, the editor of the *West Lancashire Evening Gazette*. I don't suppose it crossed his mind that I, too, had had a political career (so to speak) in Blackpool, certainly not that I had been a Red of a deep dye. At GAC meetings the governors, by tradition, sat in a sort of pen to the right of the Chairman, and played a wholly silent role. Theoretically it was a boring afternoon for them, and not all turned up. For me it was an obligatory part of the game, and interest could be extracted from the performances of GAC members. In another pen, to the Chairman's left, sat the high priests of the BBC hierarchy, ready to fall into defensive postures, very occasionally to admit misdemeanours. It could be argued that the GAC was a mere papering-over operation, its members mollified in advance by victuals and plonk and free BBC publications, perhaps flattered to be members of a famous gang. But somehow it helped to make the Corporation accountable to British society; indeed, an element of it.

2

Looking back, I see that part of my BBC experience (and to a lesser degree with the BSA) was the renewed sense of the extent and diversity of British life, last felt to the same degree during war service with the Royal Navy. Undoubtedly the lapse of time, extinguishing memories of their most tedious and frustrating features, has made one too sentimental and lenient *vis-à-vis* all those organizations, but about them hangs (or at any rate hung) evidence of British genius for something or other remarkable. BOG had regular meetings in the provinces, as well as in Wales, Scotland and Northern Ireland, and there were always representatives from those countries in its ranks. When I joined, Lord Dunleath was the National Governor for Northern Ireland: fourth baron, young, serious but witty, a cultured soldier. He was succeeded by Bill O'Hara, a successful *restaurateur*, immensely likeable. Both had attractive wives, a good sign. When Bill retired he was succeeded by Lucy Faulkner, the widow of Sir Brian. She, like her two predecessors, possessed abundant Hibernian charm; in addition was one of those rare individuals whose views often coincide with one's concept of what is right – and where they do not, prompt re-self-examination. How sad that these agreeable three had to represent a divided land!

The potentiality for new 'troubles' in Ulster had only been borne in on me at a moment in the Sixties when I had gone to Belfast with Graham Pitt. English building societies operate in Northern Ireland (and Scotland), so the BSA had responsibilities for advising its members about the law in those countries (and getting any new legislation right). The Belfast visit may have been the occasion when Graham and I gave evidence before a committee advising on the setting up in Northern Ireland of a system of registered title to land. Anyway, at a lunch with two or three lawyers and/or civil servants I made a joke about Catholic–Protestant rivalry, prompted by some (relatively mild) recent reported event of the kind. I was surprised to find it received with slight unease. Later, when the rivalry had become somewhat less mild, I was even more surprised to be told by Harry Ramsden, the Woolwich's Northern Ireland Regional Manager, how shocked he had been (on being promoted from Yorkshire to Belfast) that everyone in the Province knew (through name and schooling) another's religion, and that Catholics were often denied jobs and housing. The lack of information in the media on this topic now seems incredible. Then came the first of a number of visits on various business to Belfast when, with a pit-of-the-stomach malaise akin to that felt on the outbreak of the war in 1939, one saw armed soldiers patrolling the streets.

In the latter half of the Eighties, at the table of a small dining-club, I heard my neighbours (among whom was Douglas Hurd), discussing the media and Northern Ireland. As a convenient moment I put my oar in: 'I was at the Battle of Culloden.' I am not sure that Douglas Hurd had then become Secretary of State for Northern Ireland, but he was certainly interested in what I had to say about the conflict referred to, then a decade in the past. Briefly, the story was this. In 1976, on one of their routine meetings in Belfast, the BBC governors gave a dinner to a number of Northern Ireland big-wigs, including the quite recently appointed Labour Secretary of State, Roy Mason. As was customary, dinner was to be followed by informal discussion at the dinner-table (there were, in fact, on this occasion, several small tables). The hotel in the centre of Belfast where the governors usually stayed, had been bombed, and therefore we had (or perhaps it was judged safer) to book in at the Culloden Hotel, a few miles outside the city centre. I had been placed, at one of the tables, next to Roy Mason – perhaps because of the common Christian name or common northern background, though I was a Lancastrian and he hailed from Barnsley. The superficial mutuality would appeal to the BBC's artistry in matters of protocol. And as a matter of fact, the conversation over the food went quite well, though like most politicians the Secretary of State was not overly interested in another's life and opinions. Certainly he gave not the least indication of the bomb he exploded when invited by the BBC's Chairman, Michael Swann, to speak first.

I have kept a truly excellent note made by the Assistant Secretary, Jim Norris, of those after-dinner proceedings, but I shall use it sparingly, relying (as is mainly the case in these memoirs) on a fallible memory. In effect, Roy Mason questioned which side the BBC was on in Northern Ireland. It was failing to back up the security forces, and its journalistic standards were those of the tabloid Press. The Corporation's Charter and Licence to broadcast were coming up for renewal, and it wanted an increase in the licence fee (inflation was alarmingly chronic during all my time with the BBC): these were matters in his and other Ministers' control. The implication was obvious. There was no doubt that Roy Mason was extremely ratty, and his words were all the more forceful for being delivered in a voice that had not lost its earthy Barnsley accent.

One of the examples he educed of the BBC's third-rate standards was a TV programme made when he was appointed to Northern Ireland, a profile of himself. That had displeased him greatly. It seems he had declined to appear, but the BBC, presumably at vast expense, had sent a crew to Barnsley and unearthed to interview a geriatric, half-deaf, pensioned-off miner. I had myself seen the programme, which had not seemed to me the least biased or unfair, though it is true the miner in question (by no means gaga) had nothing much flattering to say about his former colleague. The Secretary of State was followed by the Commander, Land Forces, Major-General Young; the Chief Constable, Kenneth Newman; and the Lord Chief Justice, Sir Robert Lowry, all of whom were critical, if less jaundiced than Roy Mason. One or two voices backed up the BBC, notably Roy Lilley, editor of the *Belfast Telegraph*.

The off-the-cuff reply by Richard Francis, BBC Controller Northern Ireland, was good-tempered but full of feeling, and impressively factual: just the sort of performance that would have been utterly beyond me. It did no harm to his future career with the Corporation. The Vice-Chairman of the BBC was then Mark Bonham-Carter. The eloquence of his mother, Lady Violet, descended upon him, and he delivered an amazing extempore address on freedom of speech. Here was a case when the Corporation's self-defence and gift of the gab was justified and restrained, as well as effective.

Strangely enough, as I re-read what I have written here about the BBC, I find in *The Times* obituary of Thelma Cazalet-Keir (who died on 13 January 1989) that in retrospect she, who had distinguished herself in a number of spheres, looked on her five years as BBC governor as having been one of the happiest periods of her life. That reassures me about the lenient terms in which I have depicted my BBC service, and indeed makes me realize that I have been remiss in not mentioning more who were friends during that time, staunch and fascinating characters. I might almost write them out in a verse (with apologies for *lacunae*): Dame Mary (Molly) Green, whom I overlapped at first and shared transport with, she living at nearby Lee Green, pioneer Comprehensive School headmistress, admirable communicator with men, women and children; Stella Clark, sister of Tom King, as able as her brother and more pulchritudinous, and who went on to even higher things; Glyn Tegai Hughes, National Governor for Wales, sound of judgement, witty of speech, who kept his rebellious Celts in order and who made one wonder why *he* had not been captured for higher things; George Howard, stout, hair flowing sparely behind, exotic in both day and evening dress, owner of Castle Howard (one of his parting gifts from the BBC was a pamphlet accompanying a broadcast series, 'How to Enlarge Your Home', not a bad joke). The trouser-waists of his suits were elasticated so as conveniently to encompass rather than sit above or below his abdomen, the only such garments other than pyjama bottoms I have ever seen constructed thus. He did not utterly escape being a figure of fun, even his assiduity in visiting the geographical outposts and staff depths of the BBC seemed a bit too much, paralleled in a way by his intimacy with the highest, such as William Whitelaw, and the probability of his appearance at a BBC dinner with someone like Claire Bloom on his arm. It was a shock and yet not a shock when he was elevated to Chairman following Michael Swann. But beneath the persona of an English eccentric was a tender being who when I knew him had to suffer two great blows – the death of his still quite young wife, and his own lingering and premature irreversible illness.

In the speech he made at my retirement dinner, Ian Trethowan told a story about my appointment. I had joined BOG at the same time as a businessman, Tony Morgan. Ian said that seeing the two new members, not previously known to him, he realized immediately which was which: the long-haired, trendily dressed chap was the poet, Roy Fuller; the businessman was the short-haired, cropped-moustached, conventionally garbed other. Though still young, Tony's great business coups were behind him. He was rich, lived in style, once flew Molly and me to a BOG meeting in Edinburgh in his private jet, taking off from his Essex garden. He had been an Olympic yachting medallist, and had familiars in the world of sport as well as of business. I think he would admit that in the final analysis he was not as effective on BOG as he hoped. But he and his wife Val were an attractive pair (ever searching for a meaning to life, sometimes *via* exotic paths) who enlarged one's experience.

It was quite early in his period of service on BOG that Tony invited all the governors to dine at Orsett Hall. A major problem of transportation was involved: in the case of Kate and myself Tony was to send a car and driver, undertaking to return us in similar manner. The picking-up business had become slightly complicated because not long before the hour fixed I had to call on a local consultative surgeon, who had recently removed two rectal growths, to learn whether or not they were malignant. The appointment was at his private house, not far from where we had lived before the war; nostalgic locale. Kate came with me: almost unconsciously we were preparing ourselves for the situation in Betjeman's 'Devonshire Street W.1':

> No hope. And the iron nob of this palisade
>   So cold to the touch, is luckier now than he
> 'Oh merciless, hurrying Londoners! Why was I made
>   For the long and the painful deathbed coming to me?'

(I take the text from the *Collected Poems* of 1958, though one questions 'nob' and the absence of a full-stop after 'he'.) As a matter of fact, I suppose my apprehension was minimal. I felt too confident within myself to imagine I was at the start of a steep slope to extinction, however conscious it would come some not far-off day. And Kate would say that in any case I was apt to accept the bonuses of life as my due; *blasé* on the surface and perhaps even deeper down.

In the commodious, even luxurious, Edwardian house in the quiet Blackheath *cul de sac*, we were shown into the surgeon's study, I suppose one could call it. The verdict was soon disclosed: the offending excrescences had been benign. Perhaps I could add a word about the mysteries of bodily processes, unsavoury though the present instance may be. I had gone to my GP, and thence to the surgeon, initially about bladder trouble, the other symptom subsequently appearing. The surgeon, a bladder specialist, told me there was nothing wrong with that organ, but having found the growths aforesaid, had removed them, though not in his area, so to speak. I was taken with this evidence of enterprise and versatility: it reminded me of the episode of my boyhood, recounted in *The Strange and the Good*, when a surgeon, on the way to my tonsils, had first removed a superfluous eye-tooth.

The bladder specialist was a consultant at a Lewisham hospital, conveniently near, so that is where I went for the surgery. Membership of BUPA only obtained for me a sort of small enclosure at the entrance to a general male ward, from which came the windy and other noises that took me disconcertingly back to messes in the Royal Navy during the war. Moreover, there was a ceaseless traffic past my enclosure. I asked for a sleeping-pill but, night having come, no one had authority to dispense it. I read until dawn and after, to the concern of the night sister.

The day shift came on and the time drew near when I had been told by the consultant the surgery would take place. Though I remained unheeded in my semi-isolation, an opportunity did arrive to tell a sceptical sister I was due to go to the theatre. But no one turned up to administer a pre-med, and when eventually the penny dropped I was wheeled off fully conscious, a state I did not at all mind, an easy chance to show *sang-froid*, and obtain confirmation that behind all institutions lies inefficiency. Towards evening I chartered a cab and had myself driven home.

To return to the night of the biopsy report, Kate and I walked home, soon due to be picked up by Tony Morgan's transport. The forthcoming outing had all at once become a treat, an occasion to be enjoyed without reservation. But all I remember of the felicitous hours is each of Tony's and Val's guests having put before them, for *entrée*, a whole *poussin*. I give the object that name, but in fact it was far nearer a chicken than a chick. After a few moments of stupefaction, some bold spirit spoke up, said he (or she) could not manage it. A general chorus followed, and the *poussins* were removed, and reappeared one half per plate. The incident was somehow not unendearingly symbolical of Tony's time on BOG.

Of course, over my BBC years, fifty per cent more than most, governors (like the guests in *Grand Hotel*) came and went, solidifying retrospectively, as in some form of art, into 'early' and 'late' figures. An early colleague was Lady Avonside, National Governor for Scotland. She was the second wife of a Scottish judge but had had a quite distinguished political and administrative career of her own. Middle-aged, but slim and immaculately turned out in a superior Tory conference style, her correct, some would say prim, persona worked surprisingly well with Alasdair Milne, former Young Turk of television ('Tonight'; Jay, Baverstock, Milne and Co productions), then steadily flying high as Controller, Scotland. Contrary to some subsequent reports, Janet Avonside took in her stride what I think all governors felt was a gruelling evening at the British Board of Film Censors in Soho Square, premises as appropriately seedy as their purpose and topographical ambience. The then chain-smoking secretary to the BBFC had been asked to put on a showing of salacious film extracts, candidates for, if not all the subjects of, censorship in some form or another by his employers. The object of the exercise was to acquaint BOG with the problems arising, and likely increasingly to arise, out of the showing by the BBC of feature films on TV. Most of the clips would seem mild by today's standards, when not only passages in outside films may be distasteful and otiose, but also audience-participation discussions, not to speak of 'comedy' half-hours, employ sights, topics, language, and guffawing-accompanied innuendoes that pretty well all governors of the past, let alone Janet, would have considered quite inappropriate to be broadcast, and degrading to have been put together at all.

I wonder, too, if the sad downfall of Alasdair Milne from the Director-Generalship would have happened in an earlier gubernatorial regime. Even in 1972 it was plain he was destined for the top two or three rungs of the BBC ladder: sharp of brain, good-looking and soberly well-dressed, individuality breaking out only in a variety of plain but vivid neckties, he had endeared himself to Scotland by playing the bagpipes and learning Gaelic, the use of that language in BBC programmes being the constant topic of a vociferous fringe. Jobbing backwards, I suppose one might have detected in him the slight but fatal flaw of a tragic hero. When BOG interviewed candidates for the Director-Generalship on Charles Curran's retirement, it was agreed that Alasdair should be among them, though generally recognized that his opportunity had not really arrived, the internal choice really lying between Ian Trethowan and Gerard Mansell. During the interview I put to him what I had heard, that he suffered fools far from gladly – the implication being that as D-G he might well offend those who ought not to be offended. I think he may have imagined some hostility on my part, but I was only trying to inject some realism into the interview: I had little doubt he might worthily succeed the man we were about to appoint, which he duly did. I viewed his tenure and sacking entirely as an outsider. It seemed to be one of those cases where the captain was below when the vessel struck one rock after another; as much bad luck as lack of control.

Every organization contains remarkable characters, but the BBC had more than its share. I instance one, Mrs Smith, in my time the personable *maitresse d'hôtel* at Broadcasting House, in charge of luncheons and dinners from the intimate to the grandiose. She must have known as much about the Corporation's behind-the-scenes affairs as anyone, for no one stopped talking in her presence, her utter discretion taken for granted. She was utterly efficient, too: sometimes I used to take into a formal dinner the residue of a pre-prandial scotch, and then decline the *vino*, as not always suiting my suspect digestion. Mrs Smith, with all her other cares, would ensure that my glass of whisky was kept topped-up.

VI

GOODBYE, PICCADILLY

I

WHEN Lord Goodman was Chairman of the Arts Council
there was a move by Eric Walter White to get me on that
body, where I would also Chair the Literature Panel that
advised the Council about the dissemination of public money to
help writing and the publishing of writing. I had known Eric a
fair time: among his Arts Council jobs was the secretaryship of
the Poetry Book Society on whose Board of Management I
served for many years, eventually becoming its Chairman. In
pursuance of his scheme, Eric arranged a luncheon in a private
room on the first floor of *L'Escargot* restaurant in Greek Street.
I seem to think the arrangements foundered a few times, owing
to Lord Goodman's multifarious commitments, but eventually
the date seemed cut and dried. Was I then a willing victim? I
must have been, though since Lord Goodman's approval was
a pre-condition I may have thought the actual appointment
unlikely to be a cert – not for the first or last time anticipating
relief at being absolved from taking on a chore. For a considerable stretch we waited in the upper room for the great man.
Luckily, drinks were on tap. When he turned up I was amazed
at the modesty of his appetite – a piece or two of fish – for
the magazine *Private Eye* had nicknamed him 'Two-lunch
Goodman'. Still, the lateness of the hour made it possible
that this was, in fact, his second lunch of the day.

What transpired? I have forgotten or never knew. If Eric had
imagined that our both belonging to the solicitor's profession
would predispose Lord Goodman in my favour, this was
apparently not borne out. I was not appointed to the Council. I
don't recall being surprised about this; certainly was not dis-

appointed. And oddly enough, years later, towards the end of 1975, a less speculative effort was launched to get me on the Council and into the Chair of the Literature Panel. By that time Eric had departed, and Charles Osborne, another old acquaintance, was Literature Director. His boss, the newly-appointed Secretary-General, was Roy Shaw, whom I knew slightly through his having been on the BBC General Advisory Council on account of his previous job, the Professorship of Adult Education at Keele University. Lord Goodman had been succeeded as Chairman by Lord Gibson, whose post-war career had been with the Pearson publishing empire.

It must have been Charles Osborne's persuasiveness that made me allow my name to go forward. He was an Australian who had come to England as a versatile young man to seek his artistic fortune as musician, actor or writer – or as all three – but when I first knew him was assistant editor to John Lehmann on the *London Magazine*. In artistic affairs he was enlightened, and acquired a large circle of friends and acquaintances in that world. In person he was chubby and amusing, in his judgements sharp both orally and on paper. He would be doing the secretarial side of the Literature Panel, and I had no hesitation in thinking I could work agreeably with him. It had initially been a surprise that he had taken a post with the Arts Council and become, nominally, a bureaucrat, but the work had not dented his *sang-froid* or curbed his irreverence. 'The Arts Council canteen': was it thus he referred to a far from inexpensive restaurant behind Piccadilly? Or am I wrongly reviving his phrase 'The *London Magazine* canteen' he applied to the excellent French restaurant, *Chez Solange*, when the offices of the magazine were in the Charing Cross Road? He may well have repeated the jest. In any case, the nomenclature indicated Charles's profligacy in relation to petty cash which might otherwise be thought to be in short supply; evidence of a free and easy (colonial, one might say) attitude towards authority and precedent. When Melvyn Bragg, my successor as Chairman of the Literature Panel, asked about my experience of the job, one thing I told him was to watch Charles's inclination to jump the gun – though in fact the only fine mess I remember him getting me into was inviting Professor Brian Cox to report on the then dubious financial and artistic state of the subsidized Poetry Society (not to be confused with the cheeseparing and admirable Poetry Book Society), without the prior consent of the Arts Council itself. To me, that was a venial offence – though unfortunately we were forced to call our bloodhound off.

Before taking up their duties, new members of the council were invited to dine with the Secretary-General at 105 Piccadilly, the offices of the Council. Besides myself, the new members were Richard Hoggart and Martin Esslin, already acquaintances; Marina Vaizey; and a cultured and able solicitor called Laurence Harbottle. Also present was Roy Shaw's second-in-command, Angus Stirling. In the discussion at dinner I often found myself in a minority of one (or possibly two) about state help for the arts. I expect I was being dense, but it never struck me then that at meetings of the Council I should often be in a similar minority. If I had had to rationalize the matter, I suppose I should have tabbed Richard, Martin and Marina as unregenerated lefties, naturally in favour of many things I had come to consider ghastly. I suppose that until the actual Arts Council experience, however, I had not clarified my own mind as to precisely what I should jib at public money being spent on. Moreover, until the business was detailed in the circulated papers, I doubt whether imagination could have risen to envisage the issues involved.

In the event, I lasted on the Council just over a year (of the three years for which I was appointed) before resigning; that is in February 1977. At that time Anthony Thwaite, a friend for many years, was co-editor of the magazine *Encounter*, and he subsequently asked me to write an article about my experience on the Council. What follows largely incorporates that article, which as I write is more than a decade old, so as may be imagined I have thought twice about resuscitating the issues involved.

For several months before February 1977 I had been feeling fed up with the Council, and had told Lord Gibson I thought of resigning. He kindly said he hoped I wouldn't resign, and added (not wholly in fun) particularly not before his own term of office expired on 30 April. I liked Pat Gibson: he was tycoonish, quite a sharp Chairman, not ever mincing matters, and though we had clashed a bit our relationship was friendly, and I believe as respectful on his side as on mine. However, after a Council meeting on 23 February I felt I couldn't go on, even until the end of April. That meeting was not chaired by Pat, who was in hospital. *Ex post facto* I believed I was wrong not to wait until he had departed, especially as I sprung the thing on him in his early convalescence, but the precipitancy of the action showed how much matters had got my goat. Much of this may sound self-important, but it must be remembered that a substantial proportion of the media was always lying in wait for some scandal or pseudo-scandal involving the Arts Council, and condemnation of its dubious side spilled over in the public mind and spoiled its good.

In my letter to the then Minister for the Arts, Lord Donald-son (there had been a change of Government since my appoint-ment), I said that I disagreed with so many of the Council's decisions I could not continue to be associated with its activi-ties. It was my intention, if questioned by the media, merely to put it that when a member of any body finds he cannot accept corporate responsibility he ought to leave it. I did not propose to go into detail, partly because I feared crude and erroneous reporting of the Council's work and my own stance, and partly because I wanted Pat to step down in peace. But I did, at Pat's request, put to him briefly some specific reasons for my resig-nation, which I would disclose if the media really pestered me. That was to give him the chance of preparing his answers or comments. But so far as I know only three newspapers got hold of the story (such as it was), two of them associating it with a show (now long forgotten, I expect) by 'Genesis P. Orridge' at the Institute of Contemporary Arts, according to the *Daily Telegraph* 'featuring prostitution and sadism'.

I should interpolate here that my resignation had really nothing to do with the various forms of pornography subsidized by the Council (though on the Literature Panel I objected to the grant for a fairly dubious magazine, and believe I secured its discontinuance). Nevertheless, I greatly disliked the attitude taken by many highbrows of a complete free for all in that area, and wholeheartedly approved of the stand taken by the late E. W. F. Tomlin in two remarkable articles, 'Brothel-culture and The Arts Council' (*New Universities Quarterly*, Summer 1977) and 'Intellectual Treason' (in the issue of the following summer). Of course, a decade on, the pornographic scene is much more extreme than the one surveyed by Tomlin, though possibly its intellectual apologists are less confident.

I began the arguments of the *Encounter* article by detailing a few of the recipients and amounts of the Council's benefactions, for I was convinced there was general ignorance about these. The figures must, of course, be read in the light of a dozen further years of inflation. In the Report and Accounts for 1975–6, 'Performance art' got £59,653, mostly dispensed in small sums – £300 to Amazing Professor Crump, £800 to Handbag, £744 to Forkbeard Fantasy, and so forth, though more substantial amounts also appeared, such as over £10,000 to John Bull Puncture Repair Kit. Grants to Regional Arts Associations totalled over £2m – money gone beyond the Council's control. The figure for 'Arts Centres and Community Projects' was well over half a million. Most went to ambitious affairs like the ICA (venue for some of Tomlin's 'brothel-culture'), but nearly £100,000 was taken by such as Harry's Big Balloonz (£2,865). As a member of the Board of the Poetry Book Society, and before that of the Council's Poetry Panel (as it modestly was in those dim dead days almost beyond recall), I had regularly received the Council's Annual Report and Accounts, but I expect my eyes had glided over such question-able names and activities as they started to appear, never envisaging a situation where responsibility for them would have to be assumed. Besides, as the approach by Charles Osborne had indicated, my recruitment to the Council was primarily to obtain a Chairman for the Literature Panel in succession to Stuart Hampshire, and in that limited area I certainly thought I might encourage things that needed doing and discourage things that ought not to be done. (And so in fact it proved: in the realm of the Literature Panel alone I should have been happy to soldier on for my full term.)

I turn now to the Council meeting on 23 February, after which I decided to resign forthwith. Two matters arose that particularly got on my wick. The first concerned so-called 'community arts'. Before I joined the Council it had authorized spending on such activities for an experimental period of two years – £176,000 in the first year, £350,000 in the second. The meeting had to decide whether the bounty should continue, and if so how much. The Council had set up a 'Community Arts Evaluation Working Group' whose lengthy report had been circulated.

What are (or were) 'community arts'? The Council's previous working party, whose favourable report had led to the Council's substantial involvement, had avoided a definition, but referred to a number of features, one describing the role of 'community artists':

> . . . assisting those with whom they make contact to become more aware of their situation and of their own creative powers . . . They seek to bring about this increased awareness and creativity by involving the community in the activities they promote.

The Working Group's report before the Council had taken over pretty well lock, stock and barrel the philosophy of community artists and their supporters. I should say that the Group of eight included two members of the Council, Laurence Harbottle and another lawyer, Jeremy Hutchinson, QC. An indication of the report's views and style is given by the following extracts:

> 1. We have come to recognise that successful community arts projects have a special quality. They have something of their own to offer to the arts, something which might well change our appreciation of what art is . . . Community arts, we believe, are fundamentally concerned with the relationship between art and people.
> 2. Although the activity is arts-based, we think it is essential to recognise the totality of the project's objective . . . An essential

aim of community arts is the breaking down of some of the current barriers of official classification (between the individual arts, between 'professional' and 'amateur', between the arts, education, social development *etc*) in order to fuse the various elements within the community.

3. Community artists . . . might consider that centres like Morley College perpetuate a traditional view of the arts and therefore are in danger of becoming prisoners of their own 'exclusivity'.

4. We are satisfied that any sum [for continuation of the Community Arts subsidy] less than £550,000 will mean a collapse of a substantial number of successful enterprises.

The blurring of art, education and social work; the difficulty of assessing the quality of 'community arts' (indeed, quality was not taken much account of by the report); increasing bureaucracy (an additional officer for community arts at the Arts Council was proposed, plus a grant to something called the Association of Community Artists); the trendy gobbledegook of much of the report; the sense that the Council could be taken for a ride by at best modestly talented individuals and at worst exhibitionists or those with political axes to grind – these things roused my spleen. Moreover, it seemed to me that the 'community' was largely indifferent, sometimes hostile, to the 'arts' presented to it by the movement, and that it was almost impossible to monitor the use of public money for activities often bordering on show-biz, the amateur, the plain ludicrous – though, as to that, it appeared that in the community arts world there were no standards of excellence, no good or bad. It irked me, too, that the increased grant recommended exceeded the entire proposed allocation for the support of literature.

The other aggravating matter at that 23 February meeting concerned an Arts Council exhibition of paintings, the catalogue for which contained a page of obscenity. This catalogue had been withdrawn after a more or less on-the-spot decision by a Council officer, on the ground that it would offend the public attending the exhibition. This sensible editorial action gave rise at the meeting to an interminable and farcical discussion about censorship, and it was decided to apologize to the exhibitors.

But I emphasized in my *Encounter* article that there had been previous disagreements of equal or greater concern, and I put them in the categories I gave to Pat Gibson when he invited me to amplify my reasons for resigning.

1. The bestowal of money for the arts inevitably attracts the idle, the dotty, the minimally talented, the self-promoters – this phrase in the article was subsequently quoted several times. I thought too much money went to such people. In literature I found a few beneficiaries I christened 'Arts Council pensioners'; Ronnie Harwood, an excellent member of the Literature Finance Committee revived the name 'Egoist Press' for the publisher or magazine editor who sooner or later included his own work in Council-subsidized publication. But of all the arts, literature was the least offender under this heading.

2. Some cases seemed to me plain misuse of public money – but it would be unfair, a decade later, to repeat the examples I gave then.

3. Another phrase that got quoted was what I specified as a joke – that to have both Richard Hoggart and Raymond Williams on the Council indicated rather more than bad luck – though it was not wholly jocose; nor was my pointing out that Jeremy Hutchinson had been Hoggart's feed in the *Lady Chatterley* trial. The trouble was not too many leftish appointments to the Council, but that members of a more sceptical cast of mind were insufficiently roused or confident enough to speak out. I remember after one Council meeting that in the lavatory in the labyrinthine basement at 105 Piccadilly I encountered a fellow member I didn't know at all well, John Culshaw (whose early death was a grievous blow to music and his friends), who said how much he agreed with the minority view I'd been expressing (though he had kept silent). *L'esprit de lavabo*, I subsequently called this too-late comment on proceedings. And after my resignation John Culshaw wrote me a warm letter of regret and sympathy. Jack Lambert, in an article about the affair in the *Sunday Times*, regretted that he (and others) had not spoken up during *his* time on the Council against silly and often in effect minority decisions: the reasons he gave were 'loss

of nerve' and 'mere terror of being thought old-fashioned, not progressive'.

The attitude that prevailed on the Council – radical do-goodery would be too undescriptive a term – embodied belief in human honesty and aspiration, and the civilized progressiveness of left-wing organizations, rather as in the immediate post-war ideological euphoria. Illusions lingered on. Examples were two reports: *Support for the Arts in England and Wales* ('Redcliffe-Maud'), and *The Arts Britain Ignores* ('Naseem Khan'). Redcliffe-Maud looked to local authorities to become 'the chief art patrons of the long-term future' and supported the devolution of patronage decision-making largely to Regional Arts Associations. I came to feel it was hopeless to argue that Redcliffe-Maud's optimism was unjustified, that it paid too little account to standards and values, and that the devolution proposed would dilute excellence and multiply arts bureaucrats. Naseem Khan demanded more public money for arts brought from their native cultures by ethnic groups now living in this country. The term 'arts' was liberally interpreted, and I felt that support on the scale recommended was socially divisive, likely to be politically slanted, and in the last analysis pointless, for the conditions that brought about those arts from overseas could not be reproduced here. In fine, I was opposed to official support of a multi-cultural society in Britain; but here, too, I felt views of this sort would never win any kind of backing in the Council.

4. Finally, I believed that public money could not properly be spent on the arts without regard in the spending body for standards of excellence and principles of value. But round the Council table one found almost a morbid fear of so-called 'censorship', of discipline, of judgement; and a sacred belief that 'freedom' is good for artists, as such minds often suppose it is for children. I exempt Pat Gibson from this: he *was* concerned with what came out of the machine after the money was put in the slot, and Roy Shaw's concern increased, I think it is true to say, the longer he was in the job of Secretary-General.

As may be guessed, when my resignation became known I gained some unwelcome allies, mainly from philistine ranks.

And even after the appearance of the *Encounter* article, which put my position as scrupulously as I was able, my opponents misconceived it, and wasted space with *ad hominem* abuse. I must have particularly upset Jeremy Hutchinson: perhaps the follies of the *Lady Chatterley* decision were getting through even to him, and he had been hipped by my remark about it. He wrote an inaccurate, abusive and probably defamatory letter to *Encounter* in reply to the article – quite out of the witty and sceptical character he now presents at the dinners of the little club to which we both belong, and where on at least one occasion he has reminisced about that 'ghastly body' (I believe I capture his phrase aright), the Arts Council.

I will evince just one more item of self-justification, a letter from the Council's Finance Director (unenviable job, admirably carried out), Anthony Field:

> I want to add my very personal message to you quite apart from whatever may be said officially to you about your resignation from the Council.
>
> Putting aside your views on various aspects of the Council's work, I wanted you to know that I consider your very presence on the Council (and its Finance Committees) enhanced the whole quality and value of the debates. The searching questions you ask improves the texture of the decision-making process, and your departure will leave a very unbalanced representation.
>
> I would have hoped that the very fact of your being in a minority (even of one) would have strengthened your resolve to stay and continue to be heard. We shall miss you.

This letter touched me all the more because I rarely expect – perhaps a Lancastrian brand of stoicism – understanding, let alone praise. At the same time it revived the guilt I felt at not seeing my term through to the end.

2

There was a pendant to my truncated service with the Council. Pat Gibson was succeeded as Chairman by Kenneth Robinson, then Chairman of London Transport. He summoned me to the office over St James's Park Underground station he occupied in the latter capacity. His purpose was to try to persuade me to withdraw my resignation, but I was resolute. Normally I pay great attention to the demands of others: in this case I knew I could never live with the Council's activities. The interview was nevertheless agreeable. It so happened I had had on my shelves for many years a biography of Wilkie Collins that Kenneth Robinson had published in 1951 ('my one and only literary effort', he told me), a book I truly admired, as I did its subject. I eventually came out with this, and Kenneth Robinson was not displeased. I also took the opportunity of complaining about the 53 bus service, the only public transport road link Blackheath has with central London. My neighbour John Grigg ascribes an improvement in the service to this occasion: that may be so, but there was no dramatic amelioration until the 53 stopped at Oxford Circus instead of continuing to Camden Town, obviating a change of crew at New Cross Gate depot, where the relief crew was frequently not to hand.

I suppose it must have been after this that I was summoned again, this time by Lord Donaldson. It may have been the first time I had tramped the long and confusing corridors of the House of Lords, previous visits confined to the Lobby, the Chamber, and Committee Rooms. Once again I was able to appear less churlish in sticking to my resignation, this time by expressing admiration for the writings of the Minister's wife, Frances – notably the account of Evelyn Waugh and the biography of her father, Frederick Lonsdale, whose works for the stage I had loved in youth.

A few months later, in May 1977, an invitation came from Lord Donaldson to serve on the Library Advisory Council for England, a quango brought into being by the Public Libraries and Museums Act 1964. Its function was to advise the Secretary of State for Education and Science on the provision or use of libraries, or on any question referred by her (the Secretary of State was at that time Shirley Williams). The duties, though unpaid, seemed slight and uncontroversial, and it would have been petty to have refused: indeed, it may well be Lord Donaldson had broached the business when I saw him.

I think I was the first author *qua* author to become a member of the LAC for England. Nor was there a publisher (an omission I got remedied by the appointment of Charles Monteith of Faber & Faber). The members were mainly librarians, local government people responsible for local libraries, a sprinkling of academics. Round the table, libraries ('centres of information' was the bug phrase) sometimes seemed to me to be envisaged more as Citizens' Advice Bureaux. Matters such as the access to library premises by the disabled, were often discussed: worthy, but really of minor consequence. There was a stiff-necked opposition to the introduction of Public Lending Right, presumably because of the conjectured burden it would impose on librarians. An early task was to comment on a paper by Alex Wilson, Director of Cheshire Libraries and Museums, called 'The Threshold of Choice'. Its contents surprised me in a way. This is no place to discuss such a paper, but perhaps it is worth quoting from my letter to Mr Gamble, the secretary to the LAC, dated 10 July 1977:

> Naturally, my comments – invited at our meeting last week – are quite untutored but I send them for what they are worth. I take a Reithian view of libraries (I mean general public ones) – hoping a user may be led from one interest to another, possibly of deepening content. Ghettoization or a marketing approach (which seems to lie somewhat approvingly behind the paper) would be an abomination to me. I know such ideas have become fashionable in many spheres – and improve statistics, and may offset necessary economies in times of recession – but I believe they should be resisted. I think there are ways towards 'efficiency' which do not involve Philistinism or divisiveness among library users. I will not trouble to pinpoint the places in the Wilson paper that gave me pain: they will be obvious from the foregoing remarks.

Still later, early in 1978, a further report (the authorship and origin of which I forget) entitled 'The Libraries' Choice', drew from me (*inter alia*) the following: 'I dislike the term "multi-cultural". I do not believe we have a multi-cultural society in this country, and I hope we never have.' And: 'I would like the report to say that the further activities [by libraries] proposed should not prejudice the integrity and growth-to-match-inflation of book funds – but my fellow Council members seem more concerned with almost anything than books!'

Was one back in Piccadilly? I speak metaphorically, for the meetings of the LAC were held in a modern tower block, of institutional character, behind Waterloo Station. The answer was in the negative. I did not feel compromised by the LAC's decisions when I disagreed with them, and I never lost the sense that an author's viewpoint was useful round the Council table. And once again, enjoyment came from getting to know a fresh slice of English society, from a monstrously clever don like D. M. Shapiro, Reader in Government Studies at Brunel, to a congenial fellow Lancastrian, Mrs E. M. Waite, member of the Bury District Council. Meetings started in the morning. At lunchtime not bad sandwiches and *quiche* appeared, and a good supply of plonk, followed by cakes (inevitably less good, in the effete south) and coffee – the nation's generally rough hospitality here a cut above the average. Because Lord Donaldson had, as it were, found a job for me, I had served less than the statutory three years when my term expired and his successor, Norman St John Stevas (as he then was) wrote what was doubtless a bug letter thanking me for my 'valuable contribution'. I was slightly surprised by this communication: even three years is too short in any job, and I would have been happy to serve a further term. I never knew whether the experiment of having an author on the LAC was repeated: I would guess not.

VII

HOW TO GET PUBLISHED

I

*T*HE *Strange and the Good* tells of difficulties before the war of finding a publisher for a collection of poems; and until Julian Symons appeared on the scene in 1937 with his magazine *Twentieth Century Verse* the difficulties were almost as great in achieving publication in periodicals. From the notorious Fortune Press I was rescued during the war by John Lehmann at the Hogarth Press, and I followed him when after the war he set up his own publishing company. That failed eventually, and I was left high and dry with a book of poems, *Counterparts*, and a novel, *The Second Curtain*. I must have tried to sell these goods under my own steam to several publishers, because I remember being greatly cheered when Alan Ross (with a book of his own, *Something of the Sea*, on offer) told me that a new publisher called Derek Verschoyle planned to cut printing costs by bringing out several books of verse simultaneously in the same format, and that he, Alan, had secured the firm's interest in mine. Sure enough, after a few uncertainties, all came to pass as prognosticated. It was not the last time Alan, whose contacts in Grub Street multiplied as the years passed, not least on account of his agreeable and acute personality, rescued me from publisherlessness. People are inclined to think that when one has made some sort of name in the world of letters publication follows as a matter of course. Nothing could be further from the truth for a highbrow writer who has never really 'caught on'.

The other evening, at a reception by the British Council for their T. S. Eliot centenary exhibition, Jeremy Lewis, a director of the publishers Chatto/Hogarth (and who had once been my editor at André Deutsch) asked me about Derek Verschoyle,

133

already a somewhat legendary figure, saying all he had ever heard about him seemed fascinating. The conversation took that turn because Chatto/Hogarth had just gone back on their contract to publish in paperback two of my novels, *My Child, My Sister* and *The Carnal Island*; the sales of the two they *had* thus published, *Image of a Society* and *The Ruined Boys*, having been so meagre. I was telling Jeremy of Verschoyle's firm coming to my aid in those bygone days; succour still required. But as a matter of fact, though Verschoyle published three of my books I knew him hardly at all. At the time our paths crossed he was in middle life, a known name through his having been literary editor of the *Spectator*. The first letter I seem to have from him is dated 24 June 1953:

> This is to say we are delighted with your novel [*The Second Curtain*] and should like to send it forthwith to the printers and try to get it out in the autumn . . .

Then followed suggested terms, perfectly acceptable in the main. This brisk method of doing business was characteristic of all my dealings with Verschoyle. Apropos of the other novel of mine he published, I find a letter from him dated 11 May 1954, the first after sending him the typescript:

> Thank you for your letter of May 6th.
>
> I am sorry that our announcement of *Fantasy and Fugue* came as a shock to you. I thought that I indicated our acceptance when we met *chez* Ross about six weeks ago. I like it very much, and I think it has a reasonable chance of selling. It will shortly be going off to the printers.

Nothing remains of the meeting *chez* Ross, but I remember once calling at the Verschoyle offices (typically, quite near the Ritz) where I also saw one of his co-directors, the Hon H. B. G. Eyres-Monsell. From Verschoyle's reddish visage, somewhat watery eyes, one might have guessed he had no distaste for the bottle. After his firm failed in 1955, he had a chequered career, and died at too early an age. A list of the titles he contrived to publish would be short but interesting.

Derek Verschoyle Limited was acquired by André Deutsch

Limited. The first letter from André, dated 21 March 1955, began as follows:

> No doubt you have heard that we have taken over the Derek Verschoyle list, with all its assets and liabilities. Having looked through the contracts, I see that of your three books published by Verschoyle, the one for *The Second Curtain* was made out directly with you. We have now prepared the royalty statements up to the 30th June 1954, and accordingly £62 4s 9d is due to you on that book . . .

For the other two books I was represented by the literary agents, Curtis Brown, one of whose directors, Graham Watson, had approached me after the modest success of *The Second Curtain*. I liked Graham, and at first the relationship reasonably prospered. My early novels found an American publisher (and a small press also took sheets or copies of the books of poems), and I appreciated having an agent to settle terms and deal with subsidiary rights. But over the years I came to feel that Curtis Brown were not doing much for me, and (what was just as important) a sense of guilt that I was doing very little for them. Though some were more succesful than others, my books never took off so far as sales were concerned, and the last two or three novels failed to achieve paperback publication.

So arrears of royalties were also paid on *Counterparts* and *Fantasy and Fugue*: the sums involved would not have dented Deutsch's profits. What was more important was that I felt with Deutsch I had acquired a publisher who, though of modest size, was efficiently run, and would not collapse under me, and with whom loyalties could be established. And indeed Deutsch continued to publish me – poems and Oxford lectures, as well as novels – for well over twenty years. Then, towards the end of 1978, I submitted, through Curtis Brown, an autobiographical book about my childhood, *Souvenirs* (which became the first part of *The Strange and the Good*). With it went a new collection of poems, *The Reign of Sparrows*. I have no copy of my letter to Graham Watson, but from his acknowledgement it seems that I had anticipated trouble on account of its length (it was no more than 50,000 words), and perhaps that it ended with my articled clerk's days, thus omitting the more 'famous' part of my life. However, Graham was confident that André would want to do both books, and I suppose only the length of time that elasped before a further communication arrived gave me cause for unease. I must confess I felt far more than unease when a letter from Graham came at last. Its date was 18 January 1979.

> I fear it may have occurred to you that my delay in getting back to you over your two recent manuscripts is due to the fact that we were running into difficulties with André. I think I can do no better than to send you a photocopy of Diana Athill's [a director of André Deutsch Ltd, who had lately been my editor] letter to me dated 16 January. It would be dishonest of me not to say that I agree with Diana's reactions, as indeed does our resident reader here, who expressed an opinion along pretty much the same lines.
>
> I don't know whether you are reluctant to put the manuscript on the shelf or whether you would like to see it offered else-where. I don't deny that there would certainly be publishers only too happy to include your name on their list but I don't believe that it would really be in your interest to take such an action. However these are decisions for you and you must let me know what you have in mind.
>
> As to the poems, of course Deutsch want to do them . . .

I will omit from Diana's letter her assessment of the artistic failure of *Souvenirs*, and quote only from her conclusion: 'what it boils down to is we think it would be a mistake for Roy to publish this book'. André added a postscript in his own hand: 'There is nothing I can add to this elegant, fearless, tactful letter.' That description did nothing at all to assuage me.

I linger on these exchanges to indicate what may happen to an 'established' author, and so perhaps console the less established of his colleagues. Of course, I did not agree with Diana that (as she had said in her letter) after my school novel *The Ruined Boys* I had left only husks for *Souvenirs*; for one thing, there was little or no repetition. I had no intention, unless forced, of putting the manuscript on the shelf.

It was about this time that Charles Monteith joined the Library Advisory Council. At one of the meetings I must have mentioned my divorce from Deutsch after long years of matrimony: I do not recall having any ulterior motive, but he volunteered to read the manuscript for Faber – which he acknowledged receiving on 22 February 1979. Getting on for two months later, he wrote to me again (I omit his apologies for the delay):

> . . . I must, I fear, send *Souvenirs* back to you – though I did honestly admire and enjoy it – since I can't convince myself it's a completely successful work; and I find that one or two other people here who have also read it have come to exactly the same conclusion . . . I think the basic cause for what is, to me at any rate, its failure, is the over-elaborate 'musical' structure which you sketch in at an early stage. The effect, in fact, is simply to make it repetitious; and to give to it a superficial appearance of muddle – when of course the 'muddle' is entirely deliberate. But I did find – as did everybody else who read it – that the frequent jumping about in time and place, the repetitions and disjointedness made it difficult to read as a coherent and unified structure . . .

I thought it puzzling that the publishers of so much 'modernist' literature should have been fazed by the extremely modest complexities of *Souvenirs*, though of course I see that an author's good opinion of himself has to be discounted. Following the letter, I must have mentioned my frustrations to Alan Ross. He offered to read the book, with a view to publishing it himself, though he had virtually ceased to operate his literally one man and a dog publishing firm. I had to tell him I also had *The Reign of Sparrows* on hand, which I had withdrawn from Deutsch on account of their rejection of *Souvenirs*. Very soon he accepted both books, and published them in February 1980. They had lead reviews in the Sunday papers (and a number of dailies), John Carey in the *Sunday Times* calling *Souvenirs* 'a classic of its genre'. Alan Brownjohn, supporter of old, said it was 'very funny', which pleased me: no one at Curtis Brown or Deutsch or Faber seemed to have seen that all-important side of it. Nor did any reviewer, as I recall, suggest it should have been kept on my shelf. Granada Television made a feature programme out of it, and even with its limited sales the book drew quite a few fan letters, showing a chord had been touched.

But all this was no compensation for parting from a publisher I had been with for so long. Quite aside from losing a settled status in that area, questions of copyright and permissions were bound to become more complicated. I was less troubled about the severance from Curtis Brown (for since I had placed the two books myself I did not bring that firm into the arrangements with Alan), though that did not take place formally until 1982; and in fact the following year their director Andrew Best (Graham Watson had retired) made a move to draw us together again, which came to nothing.

As time passed, fresh poems accumulated. I was blasé about a new collection, however – the usual 'slim volume' going through the routine reviewing process, attracting the same old remarks from more or less the same old reviewers. A new 'collected poems' (my *Collected Poems 1936–1961*, published by Deutsch, was out of print as well as out of date), when it was put to me, was a different matter. In March 1984 it seems that Jonathan Barker implanted in the ready mind of Anthony Thwaite the possibility that I might be ready to produce a new collected. Jonathan was then running the Arts Council poetry library: I knew him from his days on the secretarial side of the Poetry Book Society. He was a young man with a true and wide interest in poetry, as well as a great knowledge of the publishing byways of modern verse. It may well have been that he had reached his conclusion about my affairs under his own steam, though in some conversation I probably told him of my rift with Deutsch, a topic I was inclined to flog at the time. Anthony was poetry adviser to Secker and Warburg, and it was for that firm he wanted to secure the book. In his initiatory letter, he anticipated my obligation to Alan Ross by suggesting that the book might be published in association with him. All came to pass as anticipated. Alan was generous, as ever, and the book included material from *The Reign of Sparrows*, the debt to

Alan's London Magazine Editions acknowledged on the title page. The problem of a new 'slim' collection was solved by having a section of previously uncollected poems at the end, and calling the book *New and Collected Poems 1934–84*. Seckers at first did not turn a hair at the 557 pages involved, but then blotted their copybook by telling me (through my sympathetic editor, Helen Owen) that the 'manufacturing figures' were 'pretty frightening', and that they hoped (what a hope!) to find an American publisher to share costs. Then in my turn I upset Seckers by disclosing that the Salamander Press, a small firm with which my son was associated, were bringing out a separate book of poems of mine (material not included in the *New and Collected*) round about the time projected for publication of the latter. What had started out as a short sequence had grown in Jamesian fashion actually into a regulation 'slim volume', and Seckers were rightly miffed. However, both books duly appeared in 1985 without further vexations on either side. The Salamander book was beautifully produced, but it did nothing for the fortunes of that firm, which fairly soon, like others which had taken me on, went bust.

I must persevere with my publishing history because of the curious turn with Seckers it eventually took. On 5 January 1986 I wrote to Helen Owen:

> Should I survive, I shall be seventy-five on 11 February 1987. I'd very much like to bring out a new book of poems on that date, and have more than enough material in hand. The question is: is Barkis willing? I mean, would S & W want to imperil their profit and loss account again? Would you think about this, and let me know at your leisure. Of course, I would hope the answer would be yes, for my treatment over the *New and Collected* was exemplary . . .

The answer *was* yes, given swiftly and with enthusiasm. The only fly in the ointment was a letter from Helen in which she told me she was leaving Seckers for another job, wanting a change after twelve years. Within a slight exterior she had a tough spirit and a highly conscientious attitude to work; I liked her, and knew I should miss her (little did I realize how much). What she had to say in her letter about me and my writings was all that an author would wish to hear from his editor. She told me that Seckers' new Senior Editor, Robin Robertson, would in future be handling the poetry.

In the summer, Seckers' Managing Director, Peter Grose, during correspondence about the forthcoming book (*Consolations*, as it was to be called) said it was 'ages' since he had seen me, and suggested lunch with him and Robin Robertson, whom I had not yet met. The latter turned out to be a young man with a designer stubble (as the unshaven look affected as a fashion had come to be known) and what I conceived to be a mid-Atlantic accent; perfectly amiable. He chose some faintly exotic dish from the menu of the up-market restaurant (within walking distance of Seckers' offices in Soho's Poland Street) to which Peter had taken us, possibly indicating quite a few lunches in that locale. He said one thing that struck me – that as an editor he liked to see (or had no objection to seeing) a book in its early, even inchoate, stage. I said I had a collection of poems, provisionally named *Sonnets and 'Sonnets'*, not yet thematically or otherwise arranged, which I would like to try out on my publishers in case it was thought likely to be too formally monotonous. The poems all had fourteen lines, but varied from regular rhyme-schemes to the completely unrhymed. I had the notion of prefixing the collection with an epigraph from my son's book, *The Sonnet* – 'Certain other freak varieties . . . pay tribute only to the powerful echoes of the form that perversions of it essentially deny.' To make way for this projected book I had excluded all fourteen-line poems from *Consolations*.

As a matter of fact, by the time I sent the typescript of *Sonnets and 'Sonnets'* to Robin Robertson towards the end of August I had put the poems in some sort of order. Since *Consolations* was not due to be published till the following February I did not expect any speedy comment. Nevertheless, what ensued made even the treatment I had had from Deutsch seem nothing much to complain about. Robertson's first acknowledgement of my typescript was dated 21 November, nearly three months after he had received it:

Please forgive the appalling delay in responding to your sonnets, and further apologies for being unable to say anything now. I've spent the past three or four months re-organizing the poetry list and bringing in some new writers to the list. As a result the schedule for next year's full. When I'm back in the office in January after a small operation I will begin looking at collections for 1988; I'll drop you a belated line then . . .

Nothing came in January from him, so on the seventeenth I sent a reminder (which did not for the time being elicit a reply). Then, the following month – near to my seventy-fifth birthday, as arranged – Seckers published *Consolations*. At their request I had agreed to read from the book, on publication, at the Poetry Society in Earl's Court Square, a chore made to some degree agreeable by Julian Symons nobly consenting to 'introduce' me. To my astonishment, a representative of the Poetry Society told me on arrival that they had been unable to get copies of the book for sale at the reading. When I took this up with Seckers afterwards, David Godwin (the 'Publishing Director', Peter Grose having stepped down as Managing Director – and, I may say, Anthony Thwaite having departed to, of all places, André Deutsch) told me the book was out of print! Godwin added that he had put in hand an immediate reprint (this, too, proved inadequate, and the book had to be reprinted again), but damage to sales, always delicate for a book of verse, had already been done. My old and loyal friend Anthony Panting, gone to live in the West Country, foiled in buying a copy, wrote asking if I knew anyone 'who has a hoard', or what he could do to ensure reprinting. Few would-be purchasers would be so persistent.

Then, to add insult to injury, I received a letter, dated 18 March, from Robin Robertson. I must confess that despite the ups and downs with Seckers since honeymoon days with Helen Owen it came as a shock:

I am extremely sorry to have been so long in writing. As you know, my heart operation threw everything out of kilter and it's only in the past few weeks that I've felt the first beginnings of normality.

I have read through the sonnets three times now and given the whole project a great deal of thought. While there is much I admire here, I don't feel the collection would be right for the new Secker poetry list. You may have anticipated – if not already known – that I am moving the list in a new direction, and it is one that would not be appropriate for this work. It would be unfair to offer less than wholehearted enthusiasm and would not do your work justice.

This is a very difficult and completely personal decision, which I am sad to have to make. You were most kind to me, and the little work we did together on *Consolations* – the reprint of which I now enclose – was an absolute pleasure.

The phrase 'completely personal decision' seemed odd, so I wrote to David Godwin to ask him to confirm (as I presumed he could) that it had the approval of Seckers' directors. This produced from him, to my further astonishment, the following letter:

I did know that Robin Robertson was proposing to write to you about your volume of poems and this raises a number of difficult issues for me.

I think it is very important that the relationship between a writer and a publishing house should be one of real support and care, and certainly your stature as a poet is such that any publishing house lucky enough to publish your work should publish it with skill, commitment and drive.

I am not qualified to make any judgements about Poetry and Robin Robertson is entirely in charge of our poetry list. I regret that Robin has taken the view that he has about your poems, but respect his opinions and I think it would be wrong in the circumstances, given his views, for us to make any commitment to the volume in question . . .

Following this letter (which was dated 25 March 1987), I sounded off about my publishing woes to D. J. Enright at some party not long after, probably at the Imperial War Museum. He said he thought his own publishers, the Oxford University Press, would be only too pleased to publish me. I took this in as a possibility, but did nothing about it; for one thing not being quite convinced that the OUP were the right publishers for me. But Dennis, out of good will, must have mentioned the business to Jacky Simms, the OUP poetry editor, for she contacted me very soon. It transpired she lived in nearby Greenwich, so I delivered the typescript of *Sonnets and 'Sonnets'* to her by hand, late in April or early in May (I have no precise record). The house was in the main road: I parked in a forked side-street: turning the car when I left, I had to brake abruptly for a vehicle coming rapidly along the more difficult to observe of the fork prongs. Was the near-miss a good or bad omen?

As in the case of Robin Robertson and Charles Monteith, the months began to pass without any word from the oracle. On 7 July I sent Jacky Simms a reminder, perhaps in testy terms (I have no copy). Anyway, it drew a reply by return of post:

> I am so sorry you have had to ask me whether I have been able to make a decision about publishing you. Thank you for waiting patiently, and indeed for letting me read the collection of sonnets, at my own request. May we possibly still meet in London [she had moved from Greenwich to Barnes] to talk about the sonnets, even if, now, I must say regretfully that we think it would be difficult for us to help at this stage.

Then followed a paragraph withdrawing from the idea she had mooted early on of the OUP buying the paperback rights in my *New and Collected Poems*. The letter went on: 'Without a wider commitment I am afraid we cannot publish the new volume although I personally think many of the sonnets are wonderful, and perhaps in a smaller selection would make a good book.'

The letter ended with a renewed offer to talk about the sonnets over lunch, an offer I do not blame myself for refusing.

2

While *Sonnets and 'Sonnets'* was gathering dust with Jacky Simms in Greenwich (or perhaps Barnes), I heard on the grapevine that Anthony Whittome, the poetry editor at Century Hutchinson, had expressed interest, learning of my being dropped by Seckers. So when I got the typescript back I wrote to him, on 15 July, putting my cards on the table; ie reminding him of Seckers' rejection, and telling him of the OUP's similar action. Would he care to look the book over, despite its melancholy history thus far?

Answer came there none. On 19 August I sent a reminder. This time there was a prompt reply: it enclosed a copy of a letter Whittome had written to me on 28 July (never received), saying in kind terms he would be delighted to read the typescript – which I accordingly sent to him on 22 August. Following a telephone call from him early in October, I typed out this letter on the 19th:

> I think it is more than a fortnight ago you telephoned me about my typescript, promising a decision within a few days, but you did not ring again. Two months have gone by since I sent it, which is getting on for the time the OUP took, regarded by me as monstrous inefficiency and discourtesy.

However, on my wife's advice, sage as ever, I sent a more temperate complaint. Back came a reply from Whittome's assistant (he had gone on holiday) with a copy of a letter written to me on 12 October. Like a previous letter, this had not reached me – and no wonder, for I perceived from the super-scription that it had been sent to 'SE1' instead of 'SE3 7TJ'. Even the assistant's letter was inexplicably delayed for more than a week. More than three months had gone by since my original approach. I was seventy-five, so had not a great many three months to spare.

Whittome was willing to publish, but with what he himself described as a 'terribly severe specification', which was to cut the text by about one-third to make sixty-four pages. The royalty offered was 7½ per cent, a rate I had never accepted, probably never previously been offered, on a new book. I wrote to Whittome to say no; had a very civil letter in reply. In the interim I had seen that Century Hutchinson had brought out a collection of John Wain's with eighty pages, but I forbore to comment.

What would I have done with the book (re-entitled *Available for Dreams*) had not Alan Ross once again come to my rescue by introducing me to Collins Harvill? Not much I could have done though on publication it was well received, and in 1990 shared the William Heinemann Award.

3

Since writing the foregoing, I must add a further section to this chapter of discontent. In 1988, after eighteen fictionless years, I finished a novel. Typing delays prevented me from sending it to Collins Harvill, my then new-found publishers, until January 1989. Seven months later the typescript was returned to me, rejected. Previous publishing dilatoriness and faithlessness had been well matched. But once more, with a mighty bound I wriggled free. Soon after writing the novel I had mentioned it to Christopher Sinclair-Stevenson, sitting next to him at dinner. Possibly flushed with wine, he had said that I might like to let him see it at Hamish Hamilton (of which he was then Managing Director) should any hiccup occur. So at the end of August, when Collins Harvill returned the typescript, I sent it to him. Within three weeks he had accepted it – for the new firm he was in the process of setting up. He, too, had suffered from publishing's impaired morals: disillusioned by the effects of a takeover, he had resigned from Hamish Hamilton.

The question arises: does one's work perpetually hover on the edge of the unpublishable? Is that the reason why one has never, in a phrase I know I have used before, 'caught on'? It would be a tough truth really to get down, but then, one might tell oneself, many quite good authors were failures in their lifetime, posthumously acquiring a respectable reputation – George Gissing comes to mind.

VIII

TENNYSONIAN MOMENTS

IN MY cabinet is a file labelled 'ALF GARNETT'. The name is
that of the character inspirationally created by Johnny
Speight in the TV series 'Till Death Us Do Part', marvellously
brought to life by the actor Warren Mitchell. Alf is a reactionary
patriot with an exaggerated respect for British Royalty.

My file starts with the 'Statutes of the Most Excellent Order
of the British Empire', a bulky publication sent to me after I had
been appointed CBE in 1970. Defective memory compelled me
to check this date, and I was surprised to find it was also the year
when I received the Queen's Gold Medal for Poetry. At the age
of fifty-eight I was well and truly admitted to the literary
establishment, through no effort on my part except, presumably, leading a life and turning out work that could not avoid it.

I feel sure Eric Walter White was responsible for the CBE,
probably advancing my name when the Arts Council made its
Honours recommendations to Downing Street, as presumably
it does. Or maybe Downing Street took soundings of the Arts
Council. The process remains slightly mysterious to the outsider, however long his experience of it. It is analogous to the
emergency drill in case of war (and, presumably, revolution):
on the BBC Board of Governors one was aware such drill had
been laid down, but refrained from enquiring about it. This
may be thought an extreme example of British squeamishness –
a Mrs Grundyism of political power – and these days there are
many who call for openness in such matters. I write this having
just read a letter from Gore Vidal to the *TLS* of February 24 –
March 2, 1989, which takes the extreme view that the 'official'
government of the United States is a mere cosmetic operation;
that the National Security Act of 1947 set up a parallel govern-

ment which is now the real government, for which the law does not obtain (the letter arising out of a review of books on Colonel North and the Iran-Contra scandals). How my twenty-years-old *State and Revolution*-reading self would have agreed!

So far as I recall, the intimation (a letter emanating from the Privy Purse Office at Buckingham Palace in November 1970) of the Queen's wish to award me her Gold Medal for Poetry was quite unexpected. When I had acceded, a further letter came asking me to go to the Grand Entrance in the quadrangle at Buckingham Palace at 12.35 on 2 December, so that the Queen could present me with the medal at 12.40. These somewhat military instructions were not unfamiliar, since earlier in the year I had gone through the procedure for receiving my CBE insignia at an investiture by the Queen. But of course, the receipt of the medal was a more intimate affair. Lord Plunket, the Queen's Equerry, took charge of me in the anteroom. He was a good-looking and likeable man in his forties; took pains to put me at ease; let fall a few intimacies about the likes and dislikes of the Queen, a few years younger than him, whom he was plainly fond of. Before me was an ambassador (I think of Brazil) in full fig, presenting his credentials, but he quite soon departed and I had my audience, alone with the Queen, both of us standing as she presented the medal, then sitting at a small table for a chat. I had not rehearsed in my mind what I should say as the object was handed over. It proved to be surprisingly large and, even allowing for the substantial case, heavy. Robert Graves, at the luncheon celebrating his receipt of the bauble, had included in his speech an elaborate anecdote about his local goldsmith in Majorca looking down his nose at the quality of the metal, but this must have been a characteristic Gravesian fantasy. The medal's obverse faced me as the open case changed hands (I think, unlike coins of the realm, the side bearing the Monarch's effigy must be the reverse). Beside the legend 'FOR POETRY', it depicted a three-quarters length full-frontal female nude in the characteristic style of Edmund Dulac (whose name on the border of the disc I could in fact discern). The sudden image did not help an adequate response to emerge: it would have taken a devotee of the White Goddess to find it. I muttered something in my brief thanks about the beauty of the object, leaving unspoken any reservations, difficult enough to express tactfully and succinctly, about the *Zeitgeist* it embodied, not unassociated with Yeats's Celtic twilight period.

Conversation at the table was more fluent. The room was not large; looked out over the great garden. It came home to me again how attractive the Queen was, photography often doing no justice to her complexion and colouring, and transforming smile. I was then Oxford's Poetry Professor, and she asked me about my experience of undergraduate behaviour, at that time apt to be unruly. After Prince Charles's twenty-first birthday ball a passed-out young man had been discovered under a settee, I believe in that very room. Still, he had been merely a gatecrasher. Then we talked of our children.

Afterwards, I wrote a poem about the occasion, containing the following stanzas:

> Intrinsically poetic, reading that
> Great Bahram's pedigree contains some scores
> Of thousands of subtle and elaborate
> Crosses of merely naturalized-British sires –
>
> The Byerley Turk, the Darley and Godolphin
> Arabians, comparatively down
> The league for speed but all-prepotent. Nothing
> Is surer to win a golden gong or crown
>
> Than following tradition, fond creation;
> Careful importing of exotic strains.
> Then the Muse trips the greensward like a foal
> To claim with glee her glistening Aureole.

I had been interested in horse-racing since articled clerk's days, proved by my disaster with the 220 betting system, recounted in *The Strange and the Good*. I had not read Peter Willett's book *The Thoroughbred*, from which the foregoing genealogical information had been drawn, but had been stimulated by a review of it in the *TLS*, as often by biological facts and notions. And a clip of film had recently been re-shown on TV of the young Queen, visibly chuffed, going to greet her filly

Aureole after her victory in the 1954 King George VI and Queen Elizabeth Stakes. These ready ingredients by no means guaranteed a set of verses free from Alf Garnettism, and I spent time trying to achieve a non-shame-making tone. Was I successful? Probably not, simply because of the very existence of the problem. I agreed with my son when he gently advised against including it in my next collection, though I sent a copy to the Palace.

This action did not take place till the summer of the following year. I had been a guest at one of the small Palace luncheon parties, and must have encountered Patrick Plunket again, for I later found out through him that the Queen would be 'delighted' to receive the poem. The poet's instinct not to waste his compositions was at work, and probably the luncheon party had prompted me to tinker with the poem once more.

At the lunch I had sat on the Queen's left hand. On her right was the eminent but rather elderly singer, Keith Falkner. They must at one moment have been talking about gramophone records, a subject of much interest to me, for I put my oar in and asked Sir Keith if in acoustic days he had been required to direct his voice inconveniently into a horn. The Queen, with characteristic sharpness, at once questioned this notion, on the grounds that Sir Keith was not elderly enough. But it turned out that he had in fact suffered the ordeal as a young artist: my face was saved.

That this dynastic reluctance to take things for granted (reassuring when one considers the Monarch's role in governance) had passed to a new generation was evidenced over pre-luncheon drinks. Conversing in a small group with Princess Anne, presumably about sport or fitness, I let fall that I had started to use one of the then fashionable so-called isometric wheels. Having taken in my persona as a more than middle-aged intellectual, she uttered, as sharp as the Queen, a comic warning about untoward exercise. She sat diagonally opposite me at lunch, so I had plenty of opportunity to note her health and youth. I wish I had thought to ingratiate myself with her mother by saying how quite stunning her appearance was.

On my left at the luncheon table was John Kirby, head of

Shell's shipping division, then President of the UK Chamber of Shipping. He had a chauffeur-driven car waiting in the courtyard after lunch, and offered some of us a lift. He was bound for the Shell building on the South Bank, passing the 53 bus stop just beyond Westminster Bridge. I accepted with alacrity. So, too, did Bridget Riley, the artist, another attractive woman; no doubt on her way to better things than waiting at a bus stop. There had flowed plenty of booze, and we were all the jollier, perhaps, through having survived an unusual occasion. John Kirby, I am sure, spoke for most of us when he said with frank enthusiasm how much he had enjoyed himself, confessing to qualms beforehand.

It is often said that the Royal family is uninterested in the arts. I once visited a local comprehensive school to talk to its sixth form, and the excellent English master in charge, prompted by some turn of the conversation, came out with words to that effect. I was tempted to tell him of a poetry reading held by the Royal Society of Literature in 1975 to mark its one hundred and fiftieth anniversary. Afterwards, the President, then Rab Butler, brought successively to the Queen the holders who were there of her Gold Medal. Kate came with me, and had the presence of mind to say what was true but would never have occurred to me to say, that I was proud to be a medallist. One remark of the Queen's stuck in my memory: 'What do you think of Ted Hughes?' A few inappropriate responses passed rapidly through my mind: my meeting him and Sylvia Plath, very young giant and giantess, in John Lehmann's Egerton Crescent House; the promise of his first book; the questions hanging over his violent later verse. But my reply was, and it seemed to satisfy my locutor: 'Well, he certainly looks like a poet.'

When, nine years later, John Betjeman died, and the succession to the Poet Laureateship came up, Ted was quoted by William Hill, the bookmaker, as second favourite at 5–1. Why did I not venture the few hundreds I could easily have afforded at what might be thought to be generous odds? I contented myself by saying, enigmatically, when friends advanced the names of such as Larkin and Gavin Ewart and even myself: 'I

have good reason to think it will be Ted Hughes.' It is sometimes forgotten that the Queen's retentive memory is a store-
house of facts and opinions about a great many of her subjects.

Apropos of these and other encounters one could not help
thinking (however incongruously) of Tennyson and Queen
Victoria – simpler days, emotions more easily and unashamedly
expressed. The Queen suffered two losses which perhaps few in
the outside world could imagine how hurtful: the charming
Patrick Plunket, and the Duke of Edinburgh's private secretary, Commander William Willett (whose father I once
served under and characterized in *The Strange and the Good*),
both died at early ages. But poets are not now asked to console
by turning grief into verse. Curiously enough I was given one
Tennysonian task while on BOG. A plaque was to be raised in
Westminster Abbey to the memory of Lord Reith, maybe in
1972, the year of the fiftieth anniversary of the BBC. A draft of
the words to go on the plaque was shown to me. I cut them
down to the following: JOHN REITH OF THE BBC. But I can't
recall whether this minimalist inscription was in fact accepted.

Quite Proustian, if in a comic way, the *bouleversement* of my
attitude to the Monarchy since that day during the run-up to the
General Election of 1935 when, as recounted in *The Strange
and the Good*, I tried to stop the Blackpool Tory candidate
leading the audience into the National Anthem at the end of a
'Peace Council' meeting, chaired by me. My views had become
more tolerant, not least towards other poets' work.

Often noted, the ease with which one may move through
English society, picking up on the way, if wanted, traits of
classes other than one's own. True, one can never get over not
having been to Oxbridge, say, or Eton, but such disadvantages
are almost wholly subjective. Conversing with John Lehmann,
late in our lives, he happened to mention Lydia Lopokova, no
doubt apropos of Bloomsbury, of which literary ambience John
himself had been a part through the Hogarth Press. He pronounced the name Lopókova. Of course, by then I knew such
was the correct pronunciation, yet in my mind Lopokóva
lingered, the way I had pronounced it to myself when as a
Lancashire lad in the Twenties I read avidly about the

Diaghilev Ballet, possibly even of the ballerina's marriage to Maynard Keynes. And all the foregoing reminds me of a poem I wrote for John's seventieth birthday (it became one of the *From the Jokeshop* sequence) in which I referred to him wearing a 'topper' as an Eton schoolboy. Pretty stultifying, despite class mobility and all that, when he subsequently told me that as a King's Scholar he went hatless.

IX
THE 53

I

SUDDENLY (it seemed) I had achieved the state anticipated by my verse for a good few years – I was old. It is one thing to write in one's sixties about growing old; quite another to experience the thing in the second half of one's seventies. The atrial fibrillation consequent on hyperthyroidism made me get out of breath even on the flat; gardening was rather daunting. Physical activity brought a dew-drop – often more – to my nose, previously observed in old men with somewhat fascinated repulsion. And going about the garden, even the house, I had acquired the habit of puffing my breath out through pursed lips, perhaps originating in breathlessness, but developed into a Chekhovian characteristic, only occasionally halted by an effort of will. Diuretic pills (or the intervals between taking them) caused social problems with one's 'waterworks' (to use the medical profession's euphemism). Though I still had a head of hair, much of it not grey, no longer had I to instruct the barber to use the thinning scissors. Gaps in upper teeth were bridged by a dental plate, prosthesis suitable to play Dracula. However optimistic one was about survival, not more than a few further years could be contemplated. People said I looked remarkably young for my age, but what was the point of that?

Had it been left to me, my engagements diary would have been completely blank. Such drive as I had ever possessed was virtually gone. I loved the uneventful suburban routine, really that of the retired solicitor I was, for only two or three hours a day were devoted to literary activity (including the time spent corresponding with publishers, editors, anthologists, bores, and the like); probably less than that if there were no prose on the go. I had foolishly during the post-war epoch done quite a lot of reviewing, simply through being unable to say no to editors, whom often for reasons of friendship I was reluctant to disoblige. I was not a brilliant reviewer, but I improved over the years, and delivered my copy before the deadline, and in good shape. What a waste of time! I used the material of a few reviews for my Oxford lectures, and from time to time contemplated collecting and arranging the more substantial of them in a critical volume, but such books are hopeless unless the reviewer has insisted on being given outstanding books to notice at decent length, not the case with me. Now I was more ruthless in turning down requests by editors and the BBC to take on literary chores, though still felt guilty pangs.

I was also more ruthless in declining invitations to parties, private views, poetry readings, and the like – all over-rated forms of entertainment, often resulting in *ex post facto* remorse for injudicious, erroneous, or foolish remarks. I was, however, comparatively lenient where the venue was accessible from the 53 bus route, which, as I have related, was one of the few worldly things that improved rather than degenerated during my latter life. Quite apart from special occasions, it serviced a substantial part of my existence. It passed New Cross Southern Region railway station, from which more trains left for Charing Cross and the City than from Blackheath station, cutting down on the time taken by bus. It then went through an area known as New Cross Gate, where there was a small garage (no more than a shed) that had been prepared to take on the servicing of my 1964 2.5 litre Daimler in its old age. Large garages, even Daimler dealers, turned the work down: antiquarian expertise was required, spares not always easily available. Some samaritan told me of C & D Motors: the 'D' was Dave, a mechanic of skill, who tuned the car as it had never been tuned before. The marque consisted of the Daimler sports car aluminium V-8 engine in the Mark II Jaguar shell, automatic gear a standard (I also had the extras of power-assisted steering and a sun-roof). The early models (mine must have been one of the first) had no anti-creep device fitted, so needed accurate adjustment if they were not to move forward quite masterfully at temporary stops (later models also had 'D 2' on the automatic gear-lever, the D on the original model proving too fierce). But alas, there came a time when I phoned Dave for an appointment that he put me off, pleading overwork; then, when phoned again, promised in vain to ring back – and I realized I had been given a gentle brush-off. The year was 1988: even C & D Motors apparently regarded the vehicle as beyond the pale. When I took the car in for her MOT test I asked the tester (an elderly mechanic I had known for years; in fact, he told me on that occasion he would not see me the following year because he was retiring: depressing omen) if he knew of someone who might take on the servicing. At first he scarcely replied. I could understand the reason for his silence – more than the usual taciturnity of motor-mechanics – for I had made several fruitless enquiries of garages myself, after I had tumbled to the brush-off. Then just before I drove away he said: 'Try Alan Dean Motors', giving me the location, not far from home.

Through inertia I did not at once follow up this clue. Then one Sunday – a rare occasion when I wanted to use the car; garages closed – I found the battery flat. Moreover, connected to the trickle-charger, the crocodile-plugs sparked away and the ammeter failed to register. Summoning up the electrical lore acquired in the Navy, I diagnosed a short in the wiring, probably through old age and requiring renewal of the entire system. One's spirits drooped.

Next day I walked the length of the street indicated as the home of Alan Dean Motors; found no garage. Retracing my steps, I saw crudely painted on a board at the quite narrow opening to an alley the legend: L & D Motors. At the end of this ginnel were premises on a par with those of C & D Motors. Two or three fellows were knocking about, and I explained my trouble. The general reluctance of garages to be of help seemed absent, and it was agreed that someone would come round when I had had time to get home. The young man who arrived, faintly Asiatic, proved to be the proprietor. He observed the untoward sparking, then asked (presumably of the electrical system): 'Is it earth positive?' That was a novel concept to me, always having associated earth with negative: 'I've no idea.' In discussion, it came out that, about a year before, I had had a new battery fitted, which had involved a new connection to one of the terminals. The proposition then advanced by the L (or D) of L & D Motors was that the polarity on that occasion had been erroneously reversed, resulting in the eventual deterioration of the battery. Remedy prescribed: a new battery, with the terminal connections *reversed* – a paradox as startling as that in the David Lean film *The Sound Barrier*, where at supersonic speeds an aircraft's controls have to be operated (so it is found) in the opposite direction to normal. How had he alighted on this? His brother-in-law had an old Jaguar, earth positive. I then asked him if he would take on the servicing of the ancient machine, still superficially handsome, rusting within, susceptible like its owner to all kinds of geriatric disasters. He agreed: we made a date, and soon the car had been overhauled and restored to earth positive; with an honest bill at the end of it. Faith in humanity was temporarily buoyant.

No longer had I to visit the purlieus of New Cross Gate. The next of my stations on the 53 bus route was the Imperial War Museum, just beyond the Elephant and Castle. I had become associated with that institution through the man in charge of the written archive, Dr Christopher Dowling. When I first knew him, he was quite young – son of a New Zealand poet I had briefly become acquainted with in the early Sixties at a festival of Commonwealth poetry, Kenneth Dowling. Christopher had me on his guest-list for exhibition openings and readings. I loved entering that nostalgic mix of chamber of horrors and treasure-house, the mysterious passages of the original Bedlam it once had been made more mysterious by the exhibitor's labyrinthine lay-out. There was always plenty of wine on hand, and excellent sandwiches and suchlike. Quite a few old pals were also on the list, turning up even without the benefit of the 53 – Jill Day Lewis, Gavin Ewart, Dennis Enright. Here I heard the aged Myfanwy Thomas tell of the arrival of the telegram announcing her father's death; no doubt a tale often told, but still movingly fresh, beautifully done. And there were re-encounters, as with a poet of the Second World War, Hamish Henderson, last seen perhaps when John Lehmann Limited published his *Elegies for the Dead in Cyrenaica* in 1948, an epoch seeming almost as remote as 1917. His breaking into song, illustrative of some conversational point, the plonk taking effect on his large frame, brought back a dim memory of a voluntary vocal contribution at the previous party.

Christopher's gift for coups *vis-à-vis* the famous was illustrated when in 1988 MSS of the work of Laurens van der Post came into the keeping of the Museum. At the party, Sir Laurens made a highly accomplished speech, apparently off the cuff, not in the least irksome to a standing audience eager to get to the buffet. A few weeks after, I went to the Lloyds Bank party at its head office to mark T. S. Eliot's centenary. There, for some time, I observed Sir Laurens standing alone (save for what apparently was an acolyte, a good-looking girl). Eventually I went up to him and congratulated him on his Imperial War Museum speech, hoping to bring him into circulation. He knew who I was, mentioned our mutual friend, the late William Plomer, and conversation flourished. In the middle of it a flunky arrived bearing a tray on which there was a cup of black coffee, a bowl of sugar, and a jug of cream. The beverage, unusual at an evening cocktail party, had evidently been ordered by Sir Laurens. One's respect both for him and the bank hardened.

Unfortunately, Lloyds Bank head office in Lombard Street lay well off the 53 bus route. Emerging from the party, I turned left instead of right, soon found myself lost, no taxis on call. Twenty years before, I had known the City well; as the Woolwich solicitor I had a small office there, first in Queen Victoria Street, then Walbrook, which I regularly visited. I had even been a member of a City livery company, the Cordwainers; attended their luncheons in Dowgate Hill. Now I seemed surrounded by office blocks, all of a kind, anonymously rising high into the night air, totally disorienting. I had to ask my way.

2

A few stops further on from the Museum is St Thomas' Hospital, just south of Westminster Bridge. As I have said, Dr

Spira had introduced me to a physician there, Dr X, to convince himself that the diagnosis of hyperthyroidism, arrived at by my local hospital, was correct. This done, I was presented with three alternatives already touched on: first, a partial thyroidectomy; second, a therapeutic dose of radioactive iodine; third, thyroid-suppressing pills. In the then state of the art the first two alternatives seemed hit or miss. What happened if too much of the gland was knifed or destroyed, and one became hypothyroidic? Well, you then go on thyroid extract. The third alternative appeared sensible: avoiding final commitment, capable of adjustment, allowing for possible remission of the condition. I chose it. My hand tremor, and palpitations, disappeared, and I put on a stone – back to my footballing weight. After a few years Dr X thought there might well have been a remission, and took me off the pills. What a mistake! After a month or so the palpitations returned, this time not to be cured, for the heart's timing mechanism had broken down. Little comfort to be told by Dr X that a number of people were happily walking about St Thomas' with atrial fibrallation, as the condition was called.

It would be tedious to follow my thyroidic history, but I survived the death of Dr Spira and the retirement of Dr X, and eventually found myself in the hands of Dr Y, also a consultant at St Thomas' – youngish, authoritative, well turned out. I began by attending his clinic at St Thomas', as with Dr X, but on one occasion in 1983 through some balls-up, I witnessed him depart before I had seen him. I tackled the sister, insisted she found out where he had gone and request him to return. I was not to be fobbed off with the other physician on duty. When Dr Y returned I told him I was agitated, as I was. He put me on mianserin, an antidepressant. After a week or so my sleep and dreaming improved, and quite soon I wrote a sequence of twenty-one sonnets I called 'Mianserin Sonnets'. They were first published as a pamphlet by the Tragara Press, a private press run by Alan Anderson, to whom I had been introduced by my friend George Sims. Alan's pamphlets were things of chaste beauty; marvellous medium for a poet to see some compact or unusual work before putting it in front of the general public. I gave Dr Y a copy of 'Mianserin Sonnets': he was amused; hoped the drug manufacturers didn't exploit it. Another phrase of his has stuck in my mind: 'There are a lot of good drugs nowadays.' How much I agree, swallowing as I do nine pills a day, with nothing but benefit. Much tripe is talked about drug-dependency.

Dr Y was also a consultant at the Royal Masonic Hospital in Hammersmith, which was where I went in an emergency in 1981. I had a routine appointment with him, and when the time came I was suffering from a congested chest, hangover of a summer cold. He sent me off to the Royal Masonic there and then; a surprise. There was no private room available at St Thomas', and he said I would not like a public ward. I was an alien among the ailing masons for a week; impressed by the hospital, result of the concern of one mason for another. The experience resulted in a poem, 'Home and Away'; illness starting to form useful subject-matter for the poet with little otherwise unusual in his life. 'What's been the matter with me?' I eventually asked Dr Y. The reply was that I'd had a slight heart attack. The episode served to increase, if that were possible, my phobia about the common cold: experience proved that the virus invariably resulted in a chest infection that would put up a stout fight against antibiotics. Exposed to coughs and sneezes in the supermarket – or 53 – I hold my breath; even gargle on returning home, in Shrimptonian mode, hypochondriac of Molièresque dimensions.

In the end, I see Dr Y for periodic check-ups in a suite of consulting-rooms in Westminster Bridge Road, also on the route of the 53, the stop before St Thomas'.

3

In 1977, some time after the Law Society's Working Party on conveyancing had been wound up, I had a letter from Tommy Lund asking me if I would like to become a member of the Athenaeum Club. At that time he was on the Committee, doubtless helping in a membership drive. I had never been a member of a West End club (or, indeed, any other): the advantages suddenly struck me, and I let my name go forward.

I was not ignorant of the Club House: Bonamy Dobrée had once given me lunch there, introducing me over drinks to Gavin Beer (the impression prevailed of a learned membership); George Rostrevor Hamilton, on some anniversary (all anniversaries were dear to him), had dined a lot of his friends in the Ladies' Annexe, situated at the side of the Club House in Waterloo Place; and we had once picked up Cecil Day Lewis on its marble steps (visibly worn by the boots of such as Henry James and Edmund Gosse), I rather think on the occasion when he presented me with the cheque for the Duff Cooper Memorial Prize for 1970 at Enid Bagnold's house. In those more mobile days of the Seventies I did not realize that possibly the prime advantage of the Athenaeum was its being more or less on the 53 bus route.

As was the London Library (one alighted in Lower Regent Street and walked along Jermyn and Duke of York Streets to St James's Square). I had joined the Library in the latter stages of the war, when I actually worked in Lower Regent Street, in an outlying branch of the Admiralty. What would I have felt, awed as well as excited by the Library, had I known that forty years on I should be invited to serve on its Committee, roster of quite eminent names? Kate would answer 'Little'; of the opinion that I am indifferent to honours offered or conferred. The business is not straightforward. It might be argued that I am so full of self-esteem that I take it for granted when distinctions come. On the other hand, I do not subjectively feel in the least self-important, rather the reverse. A similar kind of contradiction arises out of literary work: though I expect it to get attention, I am embarrassed and sceptical if praised to my face. When, in the latter half of the Eighties, Kate was enduring a gruelling series of serious hospitalizations, a nursing sister said to her: 'Your husband looks very distinguished.' Her answer (which as she related the incident I by no means expected) was: 'Well, as a matter of fact he *is* rather distinguished.' As with BOG, and previous service on the Committee of Management of the Society of Authors, the great subjects on the London Library Committee were premises and finance; long experience in those pedestrian areas had not been in vain.

But no more did I need to get off the 53 at the bottom of Regent Street to cross over to the premises of Aquascutum. As already mentioned, suits acquired during times of surface respectability and relative prosperity looked as though they might see me through my declining years, when for most of the time I wore cardigans and odd pants. Should they need replenishing, Marks and Spencer had become more my class than Aquascutum, for having retired as the Woolwich solicitor in 1969, and taken my pension as it then stood, I was caught by the inflation of the Seventies, with (so to speak) my pants down – to say nothing of my native parsimony suffering no diminution over the years.

Perhaps it illustrates another quirk of my character that I felt the dramatic effect of that inflation more in relation to the finances of the BBC than my own. One was not ruined, but thereafter one was going to be far less well off than planned, having missed the phenomenal rise in salaries. Had the BBC not had to battle with successive governments during that epoch for increases in the licence fee, its future now (1990) would surely be less problematical: it might well have continued into the next century its majestic Reithian way. Paul Hughes was the clear-headed and ingenious Director of Finance who helped the Corporation through those hard times: typical of the BBC tradition that he and his wife were intensely musical, opening my ears to Gerald Finzi.

Of course, when I left BOG I was no longer conveyed by BBC transport to Broadcasting House. Luckily, when I had to go there to record some programme, the 53 stopped almost opposite, on its way, in the older days, to Camden Town. Even its latter truncated route took one up by the side of John Lewis in Oxford Street, a few minutes away; and this actually proved a bonus when I served (as I still do) on the Investment Sub-committee of the London Library, since that body meets in the offices of the Honorary Treasurer, the sagacious Lewis Golden, in Queen Anne Street.

When I stopped being the Woolwich's solicitor and went on the Board, I lost my space in the basement car-park in Equitable House (an arena forming the basis of a tense episode in *Image of a Society*). But I got to Board meetings simply by taking a 53 on its way back from those bournes in the metropolitan centre described above.

X

RETROSPECT

I

A FAIR mass of correspondence and other material arose out of my previous autobiographical volumes. Some I used as the work progressed, and I had thoughts of dealing systematically with the rest in a book such as this. But the task is too daunting, requiring extensive explanations of the past; and a guard against repetitions, unlikely to be one hundred per cent successful. Much the same considerations apply to the accumulation of jottings about my early life, recalled since I first wrote about it. In other words, the more an autobiography approaches the complexity of actual life, the more impossible it becomes; a truism perhaps not always apprehended.

Many of the 'jottings' referred to relate to my maternal grandfather, despite the pages devoted to him in *Souvenirs*. I used his character and habits for 'Mr Wrigley' in *The Perfect Fool*, a course I now regret, for the material would have had greater effect as reported truth rather than in what proved to be a fairly unsuccessful novel. Even so, I ask myself if I have ever written of his practice of making cheese and onions in a brown dish in the oven for Sunday tea, his only culinary undertaking, though vastly interested in food; or of the trick he had to amuse his grandchildren of holding a coin between thumb and second finger and making it vanish up his stiff cuff, a feat it took me some years to fathom; or his pronouncing one a Tory or a Radical according to whether one cut a portion of cheese with or without its due proportion of rind; or of his saying on New Year's Day, to the amazement of his grandchildren, that there was at that moment standing in the centre of Oldham a man with as many noses as there are days in the year.

My paternal grandfather was unknown, probably even to my father. My mother once, encountering in some news item the surname 'Meyer', said that was the name, the name of the mysterious unofficial sire who maintained my father and his sister in exile in, of all places, Lybster in Caithness until their adolescence, when the remittances seem to have dried up. A few facts about my father's ancestry and early life had come down, but neither my brother nor I had really grilled my mother about him (he died in 1920), not that I think she knew much, or would have come clean if she had. One of the wilder rumours was that my paternal grandmother was a Spanish dancer, a speculation probably derived from my father's Mediterranean colouring and the celebrated turn of the century *danseuse*, Loie Fuller.

From my parents' marriage certificate, which had come to me on my mother's death, I knew the year of my father's birth, but it was not until 1985, really as a result of Kate's long prompting, that I asked a firm of genealogists if it might be possible to trace the names and other particulars of my paternal grandparents. The marriage certificate gave my father's father as 'Leopold Charles Fuller – deceased, Furrier', but of course this was suspect if he was, as even my mother had implied, illegitimate. 'Leopold Charles' were in fact my father's Christian names: the lack of invention, or plausible cover-up, in the marriage certificate is curious.

The genealogists replied very sensibly that if neither parent was named Fuller there would be no starting point for research at all, because they would have no surname to deal with. On the other hand, if my father's birth had been registered in the name Fuller it should be possible to trace whether that was the name of his mother or of his father. I told them to go ahead on that assumption, and eventually they produced a birth certificate that was undoubtedly my father's.

He was born on 23 May 1884 in – again of all places – Fulham, the son of Minnie Augusta Fuller. The father's name was not given in the birth certificate, so it was plain he was a bastard. The genealogists pointed out that there was no way to discover my grandfather's identity, unless (as seemed extremely un-likely) my grandmother later married him. But they did say it would be possible to search and see whether she ever married and, because of her reasonably unusual Christian names, trace her death.

Some months elapsed. Then from the genealogists came the birth certificate of a certain Minnie Augusta Fuller, born on 30 March 1863 in Soham, Cambridgeshire, daughter of Richard Fuller, a police constable. Undoubtedly this was my paternal grandmother. Some Spanish dancer! But what Hardyesque story lay between the country town and the suburban love-nest!

I then asked the genealogists to try and obtain my grandmother's death certificate, though I had no even approximate date to go on. They found a Minnie Fuller who died at Eton in 1904, of more or less my grandmother's age, and she may well have been the one, for that was about the date my father and his sister (called Minnie, after her mother) came to Manchester to make their own way in the world. They were drawn by a connection of the Caithness family with the Jewish community there: hence, perhaps, the 'Furrier' in my parents' marriage certificate. Incidentally, the genealogists had procured a copy of my father's sister's birth certificate, which showed her as born illegitimately at the Fulham house a year before my father. She emigrated to Australia, I think even before my father's death, and died there at an earlyish age. It seems extraordinary that I can still summon up a reasonably clear picture of her in the fashions of the First War years.

2

I am all too conscious that the foregoing pages omit the delineation of friendships that have meant much to me, even if marked on my side by the indolence resulting from a blend of shyness and self-sufficiency that has marred my character from the earliest days. Julian and Kathleen Symons, and Kathleen's brother Jack Clark, known since before the war; Alan Ross, met during the war – these are valued friends happily still alive as I write. The records of two other friendships are preserved in correspondence and contributions to periodicals: some industrious researcher may disinter them; I feel I am absolved from repeating myself or summarizing letters here. J. R. Ackerley's was also a friendship I made during the war: it continued afterwards, and my correspondence with him went on almost till his death, though in later years he did not visit us in Blackheath, we probably feeling it too great a trek for him from Putney, and not easy to find a fellow guest who would interest him. On his last visit, not long after we had moved into our new house in the mid-Fifties, we ran him to Waterloo at the end of the evening, conscious of the complications of public transport. On a previous visit, to our St John's Park flat, he had been interested in a non-human fellow guest, a hedgehog then nocturnally haunting us, saying how much he liked 'hogs', an abbreviation we ever after employed. But then he liked all non-human life. We were never asked to Putney, to the *ménage* made quite notorious through various Ackerley biographical and autobiographical volumes. I remember him entertaining us by an assignation in the Falcon, a public-house in Lower Wardour Street, before taking us to dine at Chez Victor, the restaurant opposite he pretty invariably favoured, and which I, too, adopted for many years; then on to a one-room drinking-club in the same area. A few of his letters to me were included in Neville Braybrooke's edition of his letters, but even the merest note would have been worth printing because of the care he always took in putting pen to paper, and his gift for the language.

We last saw Joe at a John Lehmann party towards the end of 1966. He had put on weight, and I told him so. There was possibly a moment of his being taken aback before I added that it suited him, as was the case. I was ignorant of the sad final years with his sister, pinned down by Francis King in his marvellous introduction to Joe's *My Sister and Myself*. The following June Joe died in his sleep.

Some of the foregoing remarks could be applied to my relations with the American poet Allen Tate. Though previously I had not known him intimately, during the final years of his life we exchanged many letters. They followed his last visit to England with his wife Helen, when dinner with Kate and me was, so he said, their only private engagement. I wrote about that dinner and other brief encounters with Allen, and my experience with his poetry, in a couple of pieces in the *Southern Review*: I couldn't now write more, though the story had for me a shocking end. Before his death in 1979 Allen had long been bed-bound with what ostensibly was severe emphysema, and I had greatly admired the stoicism his letters revealed. But after his death Helen told me in a letter that the doctors in the hospital to which he was eventually taken could not understand why he had been in bed so long. His lungs had not deteriorated in four years, and what killed him was brain damage through circulatory deficiency caused by his immobility. Mysterious twist to events indeed, quite against the consistency and rationality I (no doubt naively) expect life to show. It may be that some day the publication of Allen's letters will reveal this strand in his life and death, though if his representation in anthologies is any guide his post mortem reputation in the United States has quite unjustly plunged.

I have written, too, pretty well as much as I can about John Lehmann, whose friendship was nearly as old as Julian Symons's. His reputation also seemed to lurch downwards after his death in 1988. I do not believe in the conspiracy theory of literary fame, but the grudging, even hostile, attitude to John seemed, judging by the obituaries, to have been lying in wait round several corners. Some fair time before his death I had rewritten the obituary *The Times* had commissioned from another hand, and much later brought it up to date, as requested. I was astonished, following John's sudden end, to read in *The Times* a totally different and tepid account of his achievement. What enemy had done that? He was a great man, no doubt about it, and if one wanted to depict him as all too human it could have been done without subtracting from his prowess as editor, publisher and friend, and the real, if slender, legacy of his poetry.

My experience of Lehmann parties began, as related in *The Strange and the Good*, with his flat in Shepherd's Market during the war. Those post-war in his house in Egerton Crescent were the most populated and memorable. In later years he moved to a not awfully large flat on the first floor of a converted house in Cornwall Gardens: there, the parties were necessarily of modest size, in the end often small, the personnel sometimes largely disappointing. He had fallen back from the vanguard of creative and entrepreneurial literary activity. Like many of us, a native parsimony was accentuated in old age: the drink did not always flow freely in Cornwall Gardens. At one party an acolyte came round with a bottle asking guests if they would like some more 'pink champagne', but alas the beverage on offer was merely fizzy *vin rosé*, undrinkable had it not been for the need to get into a party mood. Also, it seems, in his later days he would send his secretarial assistant to buy postage stamps merely to cover that day's post; cigarettes (which he freely smoked through a holder clenched in his jaw) similarly bought in penny numbers.

In the end the parties gave way to early evening drinks for just one or two. Cornwall Gardens involved my alighting from the 53 at Westminster, and there going underground for a District or Circle train to Gloucester Road, followed by a walk up that variably attractive thoroughfare. It must be confessed that such a Papal summons (in family parlance John was referred to as the Pope, his residence as the Vatican; highest authorities known on earth – though strictly the reference should have been to Avignon, there existing already a Pope in Russell Square) did not cause anticipatory pleasure, but once having toiled there a worthwhile hour would usually be spent, with some agreeable fellow guest like Anthony Curtis, literary editor of the *Financial Times* – though at the last John's deafness made a three- or four-handed conversation difficult. There was always whisky to drink, if of a brand one recognized as likely to be the off-licence's or supermarket's bargain offer, and John's immobility through his arthritic hip (the replacement-joint surgery had been unsuccessful) ensured that one could help oneself to second and subsequent tots. Luncheon dates, which had become the usual mode of keeping up our friendship, were at the last virtually impossible because of his Parkinsonian tremor, as well as slowness of gait. We spoke on the telephone a few days before his death: he sounded feeble, enough for me to mention it to Kate, but I did not contemplate his end.

His generosity in non-material matters was exemplary. He had supported my work in word and deed for over fifty years; others could similarly testify. He took against certain literary figures – often of the academic variety, sometimes those who in the past had done him down, or tried to. I was usually too cowardly to argue against Papal authority in such matters (though one must admit not finding a great many writers of one's times worth defending). When I helped him in 1985 to edit an anthology from *Penguin New Writing*, I would have liked it to include far more contributions from less famous authors, and far fewer famous contributions, but I could not withstand his strong wish to make it a book displaying his brilliance as an editor in olden days.

Of all my contemporaries I admire without material reservation, only Auden and Anthony Powell trip from the pen. My meagre recollections of Auden have appeared elsewhere; would not bear repetition. Anthony Powell I came to quite late, when *A Dance to the Music of Time* was well under way. I took some occasion, perhaps a symposium on the novel, to say of the volumes then published that 'if they are not "great", these beautiful books are as near it as makes no difference for their contemporary readers'. The remark led to an exchange of letters with the author, then a friendship – kept up in later years through correspondence (Somerset far off the route of the 53) of which I have been the beneficiary, for Tony (like Joe Ackerley) is a stylist in the briefest postcard, also with phenomenally ready knowledge and memory. What an absorbing book his correspondence will be, a book because of our nearness in age I am unlikely to peruse.

Of course there are some contemporaries who have been underpraised; where, indeed, one has tried oneself to redress injustice – Elizabeth Daryush I have already written about here: Edgell Rickword and Kenneth Allott are two other admirable poets in that category. But literary overpraise and neglect are too common to discuss fully. Even the work of a writer popular in his day like Julian Maclaren-Ross may grow to be forgotten – though Julian himself has been immortalized as

X. Trapnel in *A Dance to the Music of Time*. I visited no more than a time or two the Soho pubs he haunted in the Forties, never saw him there, but have a small slice of Maclaren-Ross lore. We must have met soon after he had reviewed simultaneously in the *London Magazine* two 'crime' novels I published in the Fifties. He probably asked to do the notice, for it was well retrospective, particularly as to one of the books, *The Second Curtain* – the result of his wide-ranging enthusiasm (which also took in films), apt to be over-generous but in general soundly based (as in the case he skilfully made out for Douglas Hayes, author of *The Comedy Man*). Our meetings were not many, and I specifically recall only a lunch I gave him in Chez Victor. When I arrived he had already been shown to a table, and I was at once disconcerted by his confronting me wearing dark glasses with mirror lenses (so that all through lunch I saw my own image), as well as suffering embarrassment at being caught entertaining an eccentric, if not a madman. Much of his talk that day concerned his love, pretty well hopeless as he delineated it, for (I gathered, through hints and references) George Orwell's widow. He was not dotty (nor drunk), but his account of the affair was as cross-cut and obscure as the most *recherché* of the kind of mystery film he liked. It was difficult to respond sensibly when the conversation took this turn, but fortunately (in a way) he was prepared, even preferred, to conduct a monologue rather than a dialogue. Towards the end of the lunch he said suddenly: 'Don't look round. She has come in.' The implication was that this unachievable goddess had nevertheless some strange drive to pursue *him*. Was Mrs Orwell really in the restaurant? I scanned the place as we went out, but the matter remained in doubt. Julian hailed his inevitable taxi, and went off.

Comparing notes with others, I found it extraordinary that he never tried to borrow money from me. Though disinclined to stump up in such circumstances, I think I should have obliged if only because of the perspicacity of that *London Magazine* review. He had contrasted the books with the rather facile fiction then being turned out by writers younger than me, to my advantage, and perceived a depth more than mere criminal mystery – just the sort of points the all-egotistical author would himself like to make.

Julian died prematurely in 1964. I must have got to know about the funeral arrangements through *The Times*'s 'Deaths' column, for I sent flowers (too unenterprising to journey myself to the north London location) with a message I remember to this day, since it was some trouble to get right: 'With admiration and regret.' That it hit the target was proved by a warm letter of thanks I had from Julian's girl of his last days, not known to me: as so often, one wished the admiration had been more adequately conveyed pre-mortem.

I have related how Robert Graves, writing to me about *Counterparts*, latched on to its neglect of the White Goddess. It is curious, though comprehensible, how even fellow writers take special, sometimes exclusive, note of the things in one's verse personal to them. After the presentation of the Duff Cooper Memorial Prize for my *New Poems*, some of us were invited to go on to John Julius Norwich's house for dinner. Cyril Connolly, who had been one of the judges, was of the party. During the evening he said to me out of the blue: 'I was interested in your mention of filbert nails.' The reference in question was to a poem in *New Poems* called 'My Dead Brothers', where the poet, a non-specific Roy Fuller, wonders, apropos of his siblings, dead in infancy, whether had they survived they would 'have had my gift for/Affairs, for art, such as it/Is; my filbert nails, my moles?' And Cyril held out his hand, palm down, to display his finger-nails – which were, indeed, remarkably grained, brownish and convex. Tacitly owning to the persona of the poem, I in turn displayed my own, saying: 'I'm afraid these aren't quite as filbertian as yours' (or some such phrase). He made no further comment on the book.

I was half irritated, half amused, when one of the poems of mine that Philip Larkin chose for the *Oxford Book of Twentieth Century English Verse* was a short extract from a sequence called 'Faustian Sketches'. The piece, 'Faust's Servant', made sense on its own, but in the author's view lost much through being divorced from the rest of the sequence. I knew immediately why it had appealed to Philip: the last stanza contained the lines: 'When bladder gets me up at four I'd give/My soul for sweeter breath and tighter pills', the phrase re-calling, though predating, the couplet in his 'Sunny Prestatyn' – 'That set her fairly astride/A tuberous cock and balls.'

My knowing Philip, as in the case of many other poets and *littérateurs*, arose from my long service on the Board of the Poetry Book Society. Its sensible aim was to distribute every quarter a new book of verse to its members, and the subsidy required from the Arts Council was extremely modest. I sup-pose if I had before me a record of the Board's changing composition I could write a running commentary on the per-sonalities and fate of many literary figures of the times, but perhaps with desultory effect. Some I knew simply for the duration of the meetings, such as W. R. Rodgers in early days. Formerly a Northern Ireland Presbyterian clergyman, he was then a member of the Features Department of the BBC, and possessed of a poetic fame now unrecapturable. His Hopkins-esque diction 'caught on' with the book he published during the war, and though somewhat sinister that he brought out no further volume for a dozen years, the blurb of his second book confidently said that with its publication 'the author takes his place among the major poets of our day'. Bertie, as he was known, invariably came late to the meetings of the Board, presumably after the 3 pm closing of the pubs. He was also invariably stewed, to what degree impossible to say. He would sit upright, expressionless, still young-looking with neatly-parted brown hair and neat features, almost always silent throughout the proceedings. But very occasionally he would pass a comment, of surprising relevance and wit. (I have been reminded, looking at Dan Davin's brilliant introductory memoir to Bertie's posthumous *Collected Poems* of 1971, that the poet was the source of the anecdote whose point I failed to convey in *The Strange and the Good*: 'to illustrate the love-hate between North and South [of Ireland] he would recall the man challenged at the Border. "Friend or foe?" No reply and your man comes on, boots loud in the dark. "Friend or foe? Answer or I fire." "Foe." "Pass, foe."')

John Hayward was another member of earlier days. I believe

that somewhere I have written about him, perhaps notes for a potential biographer. His name had been familiar to me since 1929, when I bought the unlimited Nonesuch Donne, which he had precociously edited – marvellous volume in all respects. By the time I knew him he was the prisoner of a wheelchair, his disease, muscular dystrophy, not only depriving him of motion but also distorting his features, so that his lower lip protruded in the manner of the plate-lipped tribeswomen of Africa, and vibrated (if that is not too positive a word) when he spoke. In committee, and probably at all times, he was a great putter-down of others, always apt to be cutting and testy. He was a member of the Board when I joined, and at first we clashed. But, like Sandy Meikle, he possessed reason, and respected those who stood up to him. Though I suppose I was still nominally left-wing, our views about literature often coincided, he being unabashedly reactionary. Certainly his arguments and anecdotes enlivened our meetings.

In those days we met in the Arts Council premises in St James's Square, on the first floor. John would arrive in a taxi in his wheelchair, and the driver had to come in and call on three Board members to get John out and up to the drawing-room (as it had formerly been). One person was required to man the wheelchair handles (usually Eric Walter White, the Poetry Book Society's Secretary), and two to lift the wheelchair with two levers that let down from the front of the base. For the latter task strength was required: John was hefty. The later days of his service must have coincided with my inguinal hernia, for I remember excusing myself from service for that reason, though feeling guilty while others toiled. John's personality was such that only service seemed to confer his neutrality let alone benevolence. As a wheelchair wallah one had the opportunity to view him at close quarters. He was usually dressed in black jacket and small-checked trousers, and patent-leather shoes, very natty. His greying locks were combed over his baldness, the hairs on his scalp grubbily ringed: one divined that between visits to the barber washing his hair was for him too complex an operation. Similarly, one speculated about his natural functions. He always refused the cups of tea that appeared during the Board's meetings, but at some evening party I happened to be with him when his chair was being wheeled past the door of a lavatory, into which one or two of our number disappeared. 'I can use that,' he said, and the slave at the wheelchair handles trundled him in, I believe into a cubicle where he contrived to do for himself what had to be done.

Sometimes one speculated about his amatory side. He liked having good-looking girls about him, and on social occasions was noticeably successful. The gossip he loved to pass on often concerned this department of life. Round the Board table he sometimes alluded to his 'lodger', for this was the epoch when T. S. Eliot was living with him in Chelsea. Some said that John was a cross that the pious Mr Eliot had chosen to bear, and certainly, despite his editorial talents (which the poet made use of), he seemed to me one with whom life would be unnecessarily arduous. It was also said that Eliot's departure from the ménage on his second marriage was to John an utter surprise as well as a loss, but I have no first-hand knowledge of this.

Larkin's membership of the Board came at a later date. He was another who was lively in committee, his jokes, as in his poems, all the more effective for their background – in life, sober clothes, solemn features, high, bald head. I had reviewed *The Less Deceived* on its appearance for the *London Magazine* in friendly though hardly enthusiastic terms, but by the time he came on the PBS Board one had grown accustomed to his fame. No doubt continued guardedness about his verse was fuelled by envy of the warm and detailed welcome it had received and continued to receive. When I was asked to review *High Windows* I refrained from putting impartiality to the test by saying to the editor concerned that the sum of work since *The Whitsun Weddings* was so meagre I felt I could not write about it in a way that would at all match up to the poet's reputation. And I was not willing to attempt a demolition job.

My most vivid memory of Philip, perhaps characteristic of the man and his art, was of leaving a Board meeting with him late on a rainy afternoon. The Arts Council premises were then at the Park Lane end of Piccadilly, inconvenient for bus stop or Tube station. Neither of us, again characteristically, took steps to find a cab, likely to be unrewarding anyway in that weather at that hour. I had an umbrella, but of the folding kind, of too small a diameter to accommodate more than one. Philip's old-fashioned raglan raincoat protected his torso not too badly, but rain soon began to run off the baldness already referred to. He took not the least account of these conditions, continuing a conversation of sorts as we walked along. Fairly soon I was able, with a quick word of farewell, to leap on to a bus, but he continued on foot to King's Cross or other station on his *via* back to Hull.

3

New Year, 1989. Reading the new complete edition of Henry James's *Notebooks*, I am struck (among many enviable things) by James's determination to reflect in his writings the whole of his age, not merely through his 'international' themes but also (he touches on it in several places) by embodying the age in the situations and characters of his *dramatis personae*. How far short of any such achievement has one fallen oneself! Perhaps my war poems gave some idea of the boredom and sadness – even world agony – of those years, but deliberate social and political content had largely disappeared from my work by the time it had grown good enough for publication. One wished to be more than ironical or marginal in such areas, but the course of historical events (including England's and my amazing luck) seemed to preclude that.

As I have already said, my acceptance of Marxism initially included Stalinism, though before the war I saw the force of Trotskyite criticism. During the war, the heroism and suffering of the Soviets postponed utter condemnation of the regime, and I must confess to being moved when after the war I saw at the Embassy (to which I had been invited through service on the Committee of the Society for Cultural Relations with the USSR) some documentary film about the development of the natural resources of the Soviet lands. Selfless labour, the brotherhood of man – how such notions appealed in an age of the profit motive and worse than medieval inhumanity!

I joined the Labour Party at the time of the General Election of 1945. Pre-war, such a move would have seemed ludicrously timid and ineffectual. As previously stated, I helped to address Alderman Reeves's envelopes during the pre-election campaign. I doubt if thereafter I did more than pay my membership dues to the devoted comrades who called for them at my house. I did not resign from the Party until some wincingly crude and, indeed, unfair Party Political Broadcast (which I wish I could specifically recall) before one of the General Elections of the Seventies. By then had vanished any lingering illusions about the left, not least apropos of trade unions. By the time I came to do the programme about *Souvenirs* by Granada Television in 1981, I was not really amazed by what nevertheless was an amazing incident in the studio. I had to record some 'voice over' words: the microphone not proving high enough, it was proposed to put it on a chair. I started to walk over to get the chair, but was at once prevented. No one else in the studio, however, made a move – apart from summoning a carpenter, who eventually appeared from where he had doubtless been enjoying a game of nap or a cigarette, and shifted the chair in question. Even at the Woolwich, white-collar unions tried to recruit staff, and propel a decent paternalist, mutual organization down the road of argufying negotiations and interminable meetings on matters of management. In many respects I had become an old bull of the right. Of course, that would have been no news to former colleagues in the BBC and the Arts Council.

Largely ceasing (in many ways) to be a character mainly 'agin the government' probably partly accounts for the leniency often shown throughout these pages to institutions and even people – a cosiness that has surprised and even disconcerted me. Growing old, and the astonishing postponement of a Third World War, have contributed to the process. Maniacs in the epoch covered have not been lacking, but they have been confined to merely military roles or, if possessing political power, only in minor nations. Some events, though hideous, have passed off without bringing universal disaster – like the Korean War, whose outbreak at the time seemed to me to herald the end. Physical cruelty, surely the worst evil, still goes on, but I have evaded being its victim. To live in peace into one's seventy-ninth year – how unlikely that would have seemed in the Forties and Fifties. Such has been the temper of the times that one feels guilty in producing an account of life so close to the meek and mild.

4

When my son read the typescript of this book, he said it should contain more about my poetry. I knew precisely what he meant. How could my being be delineated without indicating its long endeavour to assimilate the raw material of verse and turn out the product? What sensible meaning had my existence apart from poetry? Moreover, since these pages are only minimally 'confessional', ought I not in other ways convey more of the 'realities' of my life? What goes on in the head, what is apprehended by the senses, minute by minute, is unarguably important: fiction in my time has been elaborately concerned to evolve a technique to set down the process. This side of things is largely missing here, though I admire, for instance, E. M. Forster for writing frankly about his physical decay (at a younger age than mine now) in his *Commonplace Book* – eg '*Arsehole* Tickles badly at night . . .'

But I find I can't enlarge to my own satisfaction about the business of being a poet. The other day, Aedemair Cleary, editor of *Thames Poetry*, picked out for praise in a letter a couple of short poems from my *Consolations* (1987) which she had been re-reading – 'almost lost', her description. Of course, that is what a poet must finally feel: that his verse tells all if read with attention, hoping for intelligent readers – even one at a time – down the years.

Perhaps, finally, I might dare to add a passage from the speech Wallace Stevens made on receiving an honorary degree from Bard College, printed in the revised (1990) edition of *Opus Posthumous* which as I write I happen to be reviewing for the *London Magazine*:

Ordinarily the poet is associated with the word, not with the act; and ordinarily the word collects its strength from the imagination or, with its aid, from reality. The poet finds that as between these two sources: the imagination and reality, the imagination is false, whatever else may be said of it, and reality is true; and being concerned that poetry should be a thing of vital and virile importance, he commits himself to reality, which then becomes his inescapable and ever-present difficulty and inamorata. In any event, he has lost nothing; for the imagination, while it might have led him to purities beyond definition, never yet progressed except by particulars. Having gained the world, the imaginative remains available to him in respect to all the particulars of the world. Instead of having lost anything, he has gained a sense of direction and a certainty of understanding. He has strengthened himself to resist the bogus.

APPENDIX

From the Creweian Oration, 21 June 1972

A T WHAT epoch Baron Crewe's benefaction was transub-stantiated into strawberries and champagne I do not know. Unhappily allergic to strawberries, I can, however, tolerate the other leg (if that is the word) of the benefaction and thus appear today, in a speaking role for the first time, with more fortitude than otherwise I might have been able to muster. Though further subject-matter has traditionally been imported into this oration, its primary purpose is to commemorate the University's benefactors. The accumulation of wealth and even of material objects is not much approved by our times but even a Maoist could scarcely object to the process where the accumulator is a university. The list of benefactors can never be too long for the Creweian Orator to make his inevitably somewhat invidious choice of mentions. As to hard cash, pride of place must surely go to the two anonymous benefactors who provided £200,000 for the University (in addition to £120,000 for St Catherine's) for the construction of accommodation for married graduates, thus substantially increasing the University's sum of happiness, which after all is every university's aim. And as to material objects, the pictures given to the Ashmolean's Department of Western Art by the late Dr Alport, Mrs C. J. Conway, and Lady (Edgar) Bonham-Carter will add lustre to what is already dazzling. Large sums were contributed by various bodies and private individuals to enable the Ashmolean to acquire antiquities from the collection of Mr James Bomford and towards the cost of replacing the Oxford Clinical School library, disastrously destroyed by fire. At the Iffley Road Sports Centre squash courts and a swimming pool will be built through

179

contributions from the Rhodes Trustees, matched in the case of the swimming pool by contributions from colleges and an anonymous trust. It is good news that the Michael Wills Scholarships will receive the continuing support of the Dulverton Trustees. I think the only formal openings of university or college buildings have been of two residential blocks at Lady Margaret Hall: whether these are designed for male undergraduates my brief does not reveal. I would, however, like to mention that Phase I of the new John Radcliffe Hospital at Headington will be taking its first patients next month and that work has started on Phase II of this major development in humanitarian care and medical training. One cannot but be deeply impressed by the generosity and intellectual scope revealed by the year's benefactions and if I single out finally the contribution of the Royal Society for the study of the ecology of elephant dung in the Tsavo National Park that is only because of the poet's eye for the romantically bizarre.

It is a sad feature of any annual review to record human loss. We remember here that the Duke of Windsor was a Magdalen man: the two years he spent with us were happy ones in a life tinged very much with unfulfilment. It is hard to realize that Sir Maurice Bowra, a former Vice-Chancellor and Warden of Wadham, and President of the British Academy, is with us no more. If for many he personified the University that was because of his breadth of learning, vigour of judgement, and idiosyncrasy of character. His interest in the University extended to such detail as my own nomination for the Chair which he himself had once graced: it is a further debt that he actually enjoyed poetry and passed on his enjoyment to others. By an ill stroke of fate we have also suffered the loss of his diversely gifted pupil and friend, also a former Professor of Poetry, C. Day Lewis of Wadham. His talents – as poet, translator, critic, crime novelist, and speaker of verse – were loved and enjoyed by the many: his personal charm and genius for friendship will never be forgotten by those lucky enough to have known him. Stoical but a lover of life, he is fittingly commemorated in some early lines of his own:

And what have we to hope for who are bound
Though we strip off the last assurance of flesh
For expedition, to lay our bones somewhere?
Say that a rescue party should see fit
To do us some honour, publish our diaries,
Send home the relics – how should we thank them?
The march is what we asked for; it is ended.

Neville Richard Murphy, Principal of Hertford, is another former head of college we mourn. He died in the fullness of years, but there are others who still had much to give the University and their colleges and whose loss is the harder to bear, among whom must be mentioned Geoffrey Wingfield Harris, also of Hertford, Dr Lee's Professor of Anatomy; Iain Macdonald, Senior Tutor of Queen's; Anne Philippa Cobbe, of Somerville; and Léon Marie Joseph Delaissé of All Souls. The most untimely death of all was that of the brilliant Robert André Edouard Baldick, of Pembroke.

[Then follows a mainly nominal account of academic appointments, retirements and honours.]

Some will have found the Creweian Oration unusually comprehensible this year (and perhaps thought the benefit dubious). The change was foreshadowed by the Public Orator last year and now the requisite alteration in the Statute has been made. The Public Orator was generous in admitting, despite the difficulties of tone, the appropriateness of English on this occasion, and not, I think, entirely because he sought to escape from a duty that because of the present Professor of Poetry's illiteracy had become annual instead of biennial. I must say that though I resolutely declined to speak in the Latin tongue, I have always felt the Latin myths and Latin history to be alive, and they appear, perhaps too frequently, in my verse. Because the University has to some extent abandoned Latin does not mean that we have surrendered to the barbarians who in a former existence temporarily destroyed Latin culture.

I end, as is, I believe, customary, but with no sense of perfunctoriness, in thanking our Chancellor for presiding today and on other occasions – thanks in my case tempered to some degree by having to tender them to a successful publisher who is also a copious and elegant writer. The Secretary of State for Education and Science has recently appointed our Vice-Chancellor to be Chairman of the Committee on the teaching of the skills of reading, writing, and speaking the English language in schools. Few more important subjects exist and certainly no better chairman could have been found. Our thanks are due to Sir Alan [Bullock] for the reassurance his solid figure (the ambiguity of the English language obtrudes) presents in all our affairs. Nor must I fail to mention the other servants of the University: though so often lacking in the contemporary outside world, devotion and foresight are still found in Oxford from the Vice-Chancellor's offices to the porter's lodge.

INDEX

Index

King, Tom, 115

Kirby, John, 149–50

Knorr, Ivan, 106

LADY *Chatterley's Lover*, 82, 127, 129

Lambert, Jack, 127–8

Lamming, George, 62

Larkin, Philip, 17, 150, 171–2, 174–5

Law Society, The, 72–4 *passim*

Lean, David, 156

Ledward, Gilbert, 42–3

Ledward, Patricia, 41–3 *passim*

Lee, Laurie, 2

Lehmann, John, 70, 121, 133, 150, 151, 156, 166, 167–9 *passim*

Lessore, Helen, 64, 65

Lewis, Jeremy, 133–4

Library Advisory Council, 130–2 *passim*, 137

Lees, Norman, 8

Lindsay, John, 46–51 *passim*, 55

Lindsay, Rena, 50–1

Listener, The, 102, 108, 109

Lloyds Bank, 157

Loach, Ken, 99

Lomas, Herbert, 40

London Library, 106, 160, 161

London Magazine, 32, 121, 170, 174, 177

Lonsdale, Frederick, 130

Lopokova, Lydia, 151–2

Lorentz, H. A., 33

Lund, Thomas, 72–4 *passim*, 159

Lybster, 164

Lyttelton, Alfred, 32

MACKENZIE, Compton, 6

Maclaren-Ross, Julian, 169–71 *passim*

Macmillan, Harold, 86, 181–2

Madge, Charles, 13

Magarshack, David, 6

Mallalieu, H. B., 13

Manning, Olivia, 6

Mansell, Gerard, 119

'Marston, Alec', 7, 8, 9

Mason, Raymond, 65–6

Mason, Roy, 113–14

Meikle, Alexander, 38, 45–51 *passim*, 58, 67, 78, 80, 173

Meikle, Peggy, 50

Merwin, W. S., 62

Meynell, Alice and Wilfrid, 28

Meynell, Francis, 29

Middleditch, Edward, 64–5, 66

Milhaud, Darius, 11

Miller, Karl, 109

Milne, Alasdair, 118–19

Milner of Leeds, Lord, 71–2

Milton, John, 89, 90

Mitchell, Warren, 146

Monteith, Charles, 131, 137, 143

Moore, Marianne, 89, 90

More Poems From the Forces, 41

Morgan, Tony, 115–18 *passim*

Morgan, Val, 116, 118

Morris, Ivan, 109

Morrison, Blake, 40

Muir, Edwin, 62

Murry, Ralph, 104

NEW Verse, 38, 82

New Writing, 36